Building Your Personal Brand in the Age of Social Media

A Guide to Manage and Monetize Your Influence as a Content Creator

By

George Stallion

All trademarks and brands within this book are for clarifying purposes only and are owned by the owners themselves, not affiliated with this document.

Table of contents

Introduction

The world we live in today is a place full of technology. We may live far away from the people we love, but we stay in touch with them every single minute due to technology. In the past, making new friends or having connections was a very difficult job to maintain, but currently, you can make friends and various connections every single day.

Social media has been a platform that many consider a blessing, and many consider it as a curse upon our generation. Now, the way you perceive it depends mainly upon how you use it, i.e., if you use it too much excessively without any goal or intention to gain something fruitful out of it, then it is definitely a curse. Still, on the other hand, if you use it in a healthy way learning something new and fruitful from it, then you are blessed with this amazing technology.

Our young generation uses various social media applications on a daily basis to remain in touch with everything going on in the rest of the world. Well, to be speaking precisely, not only our young generation but majorities of the people living in this world currently use one or the other social media apps. Some may be on Twitter, some on Facebook, some on Instagram, others may just use WhatsApp, and some may be connected on Pinterest or Snapchat or, as a matter of fact, on any other social media apps available.

So, as you can clearly see around yourself, everyone is in touch and are always eager to learn something new happening around them. Now, branding in such an up-to-date world where you see something new in every field everyday can be a difficult task. Standing out from the people that are already into success and are moving forward can seem quite impossible. But nothing is impossible if you start believing in yourself, and once you do that, you can outshine anyone; it is simple as that.

This book is an amazing source of knowledge for you if you want to start your personal brand and want to succeed with your ideas. Social media can be a real help for you once you start knowing all the whereabouts regarding it. Your content can definitely outclass the other people in the market after you get to know all the details that are linked to content creation. Once you start managing your work properly, market your brand with the right marketing tools and tricks, success will be at your feet in no time. This book will give you the insights of all the social media apps being used, the technique to create attractive content that will draw all the attention towards you, and in this way, you will start to gain profit very easily. This book will help you understand all the details that you need to know regarding the financial budgeting of your brand that will help you minimize loss. So, do not wait any longer and begin your successful journey now.

Chapter 1: The World of Social Media

Facebook, the biggest online media stage on the planet, has 2.4 billion clients. Other online media stages including YouTube and WhatsApp additionally have more than one billion clients each. These numbers are immense i.e., there are 7.7 billion individuals on the planet, with at any rate 3.5 billion of us on the web. This implies web-based media stages are utilized by one-in-three individuals on the planet, and more than 66% of all web clients.

Online media has changed the world. The fast and tremendous reception of these advances is changing how we discover accomplices, how we access data from the news, and how we coordinate to request political change. The principal online media webpage to arrive at 1,000,000 month-to-month dynamic clients was MySpace. It accomplished this achievement around 2004. This is ostensibly the start of web-based media. Tok-tok, for instance, dispatched in September 2016 and by mid-2018 it had just arrived at a large portion of a billion clients. Tok-tok picked up on normal around 20 million new clients for every month over this period. Most of the web-based media stages that endure the most recent decade have moved essentially in what they offer clients. Twitter, for instance, did not permit clients to transfer recordings or pictures in the first place. Since 2011 this is conceivable and today over half of the substance saw on Twitter incorporates pictures and recordings.

Youngsters will in general utilize online media much of their time. Indeed, in rich nations, where admittance to the web is almost very common, by far most of youthful grown-ups use it. The expansion in web-based media use throughout the most recent decade has; obviously, meet up with a huge expansion in the measure of time that individuals spend online.

The ascent of web-based media is a phenomenal illustration of how rapidly and definitely social practices can change. Something that is today essential for the regular day to day existence of 33% of the total populace was unimaginable in the past. Quick changes like those achieved by web-based media consistently flash feelings of trepidation about conceivable negative impacts. Explicitly with regards to online media, a key inquiry is whether these new correspondence advancements are negatively affecting our emotional well-being.

1.1 Introduction to Social Media

Data and correspondence innovation has changed quickly in the course of recent years with a key advancement being the development of web-based media. The movement of progress is quickening. For instance, the improvement of portable innovation has assumed a significant function in molding the effect of web-based media. Over the globe, cell phones dominate in terms of total minutes spent online. This puts the means to connect anywhere, at any time on any device in everyone's hands.

Web-based media assumes a significant role in the present life, web-based media are electronic online devices that empower individuals find and learn new data, share thoughts, interface with new individuals and associations. It has changed the way individuals carry on with their life today; it has made correspondence a lot simpler. It permits the trading of client created content like information, pictures, and recordings. Web-based media stages may come in various structures, for example, online journals, business discussions, digital broadcasts, microblogs, photograph sharing, administration audit, weblogs and so forth.

Studies have demonstrated that a significant decent number of individuals invest 25% of their energy on long range interpersonal communication stages, this goes further to show how applicable and famous web-based media stages have become lately.

The significance of web-based media can be found in many fields, for example, business, amusement, food, government assistance, lifestyle, etc. It is essential to any business in light of the fact that as a business person you own an image and with the assistance of web-based media organizing different events, staying in contact with their clients and getting significant data about them can become very easy. The greater parts of the business person and advertisers have effectively utilized this stage with regards to arriving at expected customers.

Organizations have acknowledged they can utilize web-based media to create bits of knowledge, animate interest, and create a focus on themselves. This is significant in conventional block and-engine organizations, and, clearly, in the realm of internet business.

Numerous investigations recommend executing informal communities inside the working environment can reinforce information sharing. The result is to improve project management activities and enable the spread of specialized knowledge. Fully implementing social technologies in the workplace removes boundaries, eliminates silos, and can raise interaction and help create more highly skilled and knowledgeable workers.

It has been said that data is power. Without the methods for disseminating data, individuals cannot bridle the force. One sure effect of web-based media is in the dissemination of data in this day and age. Various social media platforms, for example, Facebook, LinkedIn, Twitter and others have made it conceivable to get to data at the snap of a button.

1.2 Importance of Social Media in the World we live in today

Web-based media is characterized by its intuitiveness, connectedness, and client produced content. In the present society, the utilization of online media has become a fundamental day by day action. Online media is regularly utilized for social connection and admittance to news and data. It is a significant specialized device with others locally and around the world, just as to share, make, and spread data.

Web-based media can impact buyer's buy choices through audits, showcasing strategies and promoting. Basically, online media incomprehensibly impacts our capacity to impart, structure connections, access and spread data, and to show up at the best choice. Maybe the most persuasive web-based media instrument is long range informal communication destinations. Facebook, Twitter, Tumblr, Blogger, LinkedIn, and Google + are for the most part recognizable names to the vast majority of the society; which may be either dynamic online media client or not.

Nearly everybody from the ages of 13 to 64 has a Facebook account. These interpersonal interaction destinations can be utilized to interface individuals around the world. This implies that conferences can be led globally by means of Google Hangouts or old companions can reconnect. For organizations, schools, and different gatherings, the correspondence prospects are perpetual.

These long-range interpersonal communication destinations have progressively developed past close to home use. As of late, businesses have started utilizing informal communication destinations to analyze the foundation of their imminent competitors, just as to have interviews through Facebook or other web-based media innovation apparatuses.

Groups can plan virtual gatherings or conceptualize together in any event, when they cannot truly meet. This facilitates the booking pressures for school tasks and executive gatherings. It is implied that we as a general public have become dependent and reliant on long range interpersonal communication locales. Generally speaking, we depend on interpersonal organizations for availability and essential correspondence in this day and age. Following are some reasons why social media is important:

- Most likely, all of your competitors will either already have an online presence or plan to incorporate social media marketing strategies into their businesses. Even if you and your competitors are not currently implementing a social media strategy, just know that it is likely that soon your competitors will begin to do so any day.

- Focusing on clients from everywhere in the world assists you with expanding deals and makes it almost certain that your more aggressive deals targets will be met. Administration situated organizations can particularly exploit the almost cost-free climate of online media that can give a worldwide presence.

- By examining online media technique open doors for clients to give criticism just as open doors for direct exchange with a corporate delegate over any social media account can be conceivable. Web-based media endeavors give organizations a computerized character and give an extra part to compelling marking strategies.

- You need to get with your customers. Criticism is the soul of any business and online media encourages you discover what your clients need to state about you. Whenever you have imparted about your business and made a deal, you need to hear what you can and ought to do to improve your administration.

- Another cool thing is that fruitful help stories and fulfilled clients have a higher probability of getting out the word to others all alone by getting your organization a presence and character via web-based media networks. Web-based media is your key to two ways correspondence and proceeded with proficient achievement.

- In the event that you have recently begun your business, be it a café, clothing shop, or any other organization, paying little mind to the fie you are working in, you can diminish tension on funds from advertising companies by taking your marketing on the web. Internet promoting efforts are substantially less costly then print media crusades that regularly consolidate show publicizing in neighborhood papers just as public periodicals. Another favorable position of online missions over print has to do with time affectability where commercials bought in papers and magazines have a restricted viable presentation period. Online ads are perceptible to clients as long as organizations want them to be with time spans enduring from days to years.

- Geological limits cannot prevent online media from contacting individuals, possibilities, and clients over the globe. Anyone who has online presence can be focused on. On the off chance that you are head tracker or a counseling firm, would it not be ideal to extend your span on a worldwide scale and to begin growing your business and piece of the pie by beginning to serve clients from everywhere the world.

The potential outcomes are apparently inestimable for online media. It is exceptional for individuals to go a day without utilizing or alluding to online media. Regardless of whether it is utilized for conveying, learning, or dynamic, online media is digging in for the long haul and will keep on influencing our general public.

1.3 Different Social Media Platforms

Regardless of whether you are a prepared online media advertiser, an advertiser hoping to wander into web-based media promoting, or an entrepreneur hoping to succeed via web-based media, it is useful to know the most famous web-based media destinations around the world that you can target. This will permit you to amplify your image reach via web-based media, draw in with the correct individuals, and accomplish your web-based media objectives.

Obviously, it is not just about the size of the online media destinations. It is additionally whether the online media website is a correct fit for your business and you or not. Does it fit your image picture? Is your intended interest group utilizing that online media webpage? What number of online media locales would you be able to oversee at a single time? To make things simpler for you, following are some social media platforms that you can use to reach out to your clients and start branding:

1. **YouTube**

YouTube is a video-sharing stage where clients watch a billion hour of recordings consistently. To begin, you can make a YouTube channel for your company where you can transfer recordings for your endorsers of view, similar to, remark, and share. Other than being the second greatest web-based media website, YouTube is likewise regularly known as the second biggest web index after Google. At long last, you can likewise promote on YouTube to expand your range on the stage.

2. Instagram

Instagram is a photograph and video sharing online media application. It permits you to share a wide scope of substance, for example, photographs, recordings, stories, and live recordings. It has likewise as of late dispatched IGTV for longer-structure recordings. As a brand, you can have an Instagram business profile, which will give you rich examination of your profile and presents and the capacity on time Instagram posts utilizing third-party instruments.

3. Tik Tok

Tik Tok is a rising music video informal organization. It was the world's most downloaded application in the main quarter of 2018, beating Facebook, Instagram, and other web-based media applications. The underlying impression is that it would seem that Instagram for short music recordings. Clients can record recordings as long as 60 seconds, alter them, and add music and embellishments. While it is generally famous in Asia, its notoriety is also spreading towards the west.

4. Twitter

Twitter is a web-based media webpage for news, amusement, sports, governmental issues, and the sky is the limit from there. What makes Twitter not the same as most other web-based media destinations is that it has a solid accentuation on ongoing data i.e., things that are going on the present moment. Another extraordinary trait of Twitter is that it just permits 280 characters in a tweet, dissimilar to most online media locales that have a lot higher cutoff.

Twitter is likewise regularly utilized as a client care channel. As indicated by publicists on Twitter, in excess of 80% of social client assistance demands occur on Twitter. Quick and in some cases irate, certain organizations truly blossom with Twitter.

If your business is identified with diversion, sports, governmental issues, or showcasing, you remain to procure colossal commitment on Twitter. On Twitter, brands have an occasion to art and sharpen their voice there is space to be astute and friendly notwithstanding useful and supportive.

5. LinkedIn

LinkedIn is currently something beyond a resume and pursuit of employment site. It has advanced into an expert online media website where industry specialists share content, network with each other, and construct their own image. It has likewise become a spot for organizations to build up their idea administration and authority in their industry and pull in ability to their organization. LinkedIn likewise offers promoting openings, for example, sending personalized ads to LinkedIn inboxes, and displaying ads by the side of the site.

6. Facebook

Facebook is the greatest web-based media website around, with in excess of two billion individuals utilizing it consistently. That is right around 33% of the total populace. There are in excess of 65 million organizations utilizing Facebook pages and in excess of 6,000,000 publicists effectively advancing their business on Facebook, which makes it a truly an amazing application to use if you need to have a presence via online media. It is anything but difficult to begin on Facebook in light of the fact that practically all substance design works incredible on Facebook i.e., text, pictures, recordings, live recordings, and stories. However, note that the Facebook algorithm organizes content that sparks discussions and significant connections between individuals, particularly those from loved ones.

This OG web-based media network is reliable, and regardless of your industry, there is a space for you on Facebook. A portion of the main ventures on Facebook incorporate monetary administrations, internet business, retail, gaming, amusement, media, telecom, innovation, shopper merchandise, and car organizations. While the news feed progressively stifles business posts, there are still approaches to reinforce commitment without putting resources into advertisements. Think about joining (or making) gatherings, utilizing a Facebook Messenger chat box, or utilizing live video to up your commitment.

7. Snapchat

Snapchat is a social media app that focuses on sharing photos and short videos (as known as snaps) between friends. It made the Stories format popular, which eventually proliferated on other social media platforms like Instagram. But the rise of Instagram Stories seemed to have hindered Snapchat's growth and marketers' interest in using Snapchat for their brands in general. In the event that your objective target is young, you certainly need to get in on Snapchat. The most dynamic clients on Snapchat are 13-year-olds, and they are going through as much as thirty minutes every day on the application. Snapchat is an asylum for client produced content, in the background recordings, selective offers, and influencer takeovers.

8. Pinterest

Pinterest is a place where people go to discover new things and be inspired, quite unlike most social media sites where engagement is the primary focus. According to Pinterest, 78 percent of users say that content on Pinterest from brands are useful. This gives your brand a unique opportunity to shape their purchasing decisions. As Pinterest users want to be inspired to try or buy new things, having a presence on Pinterest could help put your brand on their minds.

This online model for peer business has gotten suitable and mainstream as of late as individuals began believing on the web audits and feeling good utilizing them to measure the standing and unwavering quality of merchants and service providers. While most marketers will find these networks too specifically targeted or restrictive, if you happen to provide the kind of product or administration that is exchanged on a specific organization, you should investigate it as another channel to produce leads and deals.

1.4 Social Media Marketing

Online media advertising is a type of web promoting that includes making and sharing substance via web-based media networks to accomplish your showcasing and marking objectives. Online media showcasing incorporates exercises like posting text and picture updates, recordings, and other substance that drives crowd commitment, just as paid web-based media promoting. The significant web-based media stages are Facebook, Instagram, Twitter, LinkedIn, Pinterest, YouTube, and Snapchat.

There is likewise a scope of online media the board devices that assist organizations with capitalizing on the web-based media stages recorded previously. Regardless of whether you need to construct a brand or develop your business, you need to be marketing.

Before you start making web-based media showcasing efforts, think about your business objectives. Beginning an online media advertising effort without a social system as a main priority resembles meandering around backwoods without a guide, you may have a great time, yet you will presumably get lost. Following are the benefits of social media marketing:

1. A solid online media showcasing procedure will create discussion about your image, items, and accomplices. Social listening is the demonstration of observing social discussions around specific subjects. It encourages you comprehend what is critical to your crowd and distinguish patterns your intended interest group is following. You will find out about what they are battling with, which can assist you with making content tending to those problem areas. You can likewise distinguish the tone and language that your intended interest group employments.

2. Picking up brand acknowledgment is one of any business most significant showcasing objectives. That is on the grounds that purchasers need to purchase brands they perceive. Fortunately, online media takes into account simple and viable brand building. Online media has an advantage over conventional media in light of the fact that it can get your image before individuals considerably more rapidly and without any problem.

3. Utilizing online media is an extraordinary method to share your image's main goal and offer stories. Compelling stories can greatly affect your brand's picture. They can be straightforward or broad relying upon what you think will be best.

4. Crowd research is like social tuning in. It looks through the watchwords your crowd will utilize, yet it is more centered around your particular item. You can utilize online media to accumulate this data. To see the bits of knowledge on your Facebook page, basically go to the page that you are the administrator of and they will be close to your cover photograph. Twitter will have a choice to see the bits of knowledge of each tweet you post at the lower part of each tweet.

5. Clients currently anticipate that organizations should deal with their solicitations through online media. A solid interest in client care can construct important connections between your organization and your clients. Furthermore, with online media, the test of client assistance stays as requesting as it had previously. Online media takes into consideration quick communication and client criticism. Organizations can likewise react to their clients immediately.

6. Web-based media advertising can help with sending clients straightforwardly to your webpage. It is improbable that the entirety of your traffic will come through web crawlers. Online media channels take into consideration more assorted inbound traffic streams. In spite of the fact that informal communities are incredible for getting traffic to your site, you need to consider what to post as well as how frequently to post. You would prefer not to turn into that tyrannical advertiser, or you will kill your clients.

7. Clients follow and connect with the brands they appreciate. Yet it is fascinating that 53% of clients who follow your business are probably going to be faithful to your business explicitly. It is a conspicuous direct relationship i.e., if clients follow you, they are bound to pick you versus your opposition. Besides, on the off chance that they are faithful clients, they will increment your traffic.

8. Online media can indirectly affect SEO. It is acceptable to follow a set timetable for posting your substance. This will assist you with guaranteeing that your substance is not just posted during a period that is best,

it will likewise give you an opportunity to alter your content to assist you with your SEO.

9. It is allowed to make web-based media profiles and post natural substance. For a few, that might sufficiently be, and the nature of the content may advance. Although, in the event that you would prefer to go the additional mile and advance it further, paying for advancement will help increment presentation. You need to set up a mission, and they will work with your financial plan. That implies you will have an enormous ROI and you will utilize your showcasing financial plan in a powerful manner.

10. Retargeting is a great device for web-based media advertising. For the most part just 2% of clients will really buy something during their first visit to your site. Publicizing can help arrive at that other 98%. One approach to do that is to run retargeting promotions. Retargeting works by keeping a rundown of individuals who visit your site and putting unknown treats inside their program. When they visit an online media website, a retargeting administration at that point shows the advertisements. This takes into consideration your business to be according to the client past exactly when they are on your site.

11. Web-based media can hugely affect making promotions viral. We are all acquainted with viral advertisements; simply go for a stroll through a world of fond memories and investigate a portion of these extraordinary viral missions. Truth be told, that is the place where the greater part of those promotions is shared. These ads can be placed anywhere on social media and can direct the customer to your site. The trick is to make sure that your site keeps the customer engaged enough to want to continue to purchase the product.

12. Advance your content, and you will succeed. However, what are the most ideal approaches to do that? We should investigate the things that have any kind of effect, for example, features, having a picture, and the hour of the post. Every one of these things are significant and must be thought about when composing an online media message. The main thing to remember recorded as a hard copy your messages is to be imaginative. You need to ensure that you are posting unique content. The hashtag is an amazing asset that can associate a gathering of similarly invested people through web-based media. It is a straightforward method to extraordinarily build your brand.

13. Web-based media is truly outstanding and simplest methods of keeping your clients refreshed with your new items or forthcoming occasions. If your business makes a tremendous declaration about another item or an energizing occasion, it will get on and get individuals energized.

When you have more assets to become your online media promoting, a region that you can consider is web-based media publicizing. Web-based media promotions permit you to contact a more extensive crowd than the individuals who are following you. Online media promoting stages are so incredible these days that you can determine precisely who to show your advertisements to. You can make target crowds dependent on their socioeconomics, interests, practices, and that is only the tip of the iceberg. When you are running numerous web-based media publicizing efforts without a moment's delay, you can consider utilizing a web-based media promoting instrument to make mass changes, robotize processes, and enhance your advertisements.

Chapter 2: Content Creation

Content creation is the way toward recognizing another subject you need to write on, choosing which structure you need the content to take, formalizing your procedure, and afterward really delivering it. Moreover, most content creation measures include careful rounds of alters with different partners before content is prepared to publish. Since content can take numerous structures i.e., blogs, video, eBook, Tweet, infographic, notice, to give some examples. The content creation measure is nuanced and not generally as straightforward as it would appear. Yet, doing it well can really affect your business. Truth be told, recent examination demonstrates that making quality instructive content makes clients 131% more likely to purchase from your business.

Making extraordinary content begins with a settled cycle. We will walk you through the content creation from the beginning to end, and exhibit how making extraordinary content can help your crowds and clients discover arrangements and answers to their issues.

Ideas for content can emerge out of an assortment of spots, both from inside your content group, from your clients, from different partners in your organization, from new information, or from something that motivates you. And, depending on the goal of the piece of content, deciding the correct angle you should take on a specific topic can prove challenging. For instance, in case you are entrusted with making content that includes a new product feature, you may have a baseline idea of what you need to produce. But if your task is broader, for example, write a piece of early-stage content that will drive organic traffic to your website, then you may need to investigate other methods of coming up with content ideas. Following are some techniques you can use to create ideas for your content:

- Asking your clients may seem like a basic method to get a thought, yet frequently there are unanswered inquiries they have about your item or your space that you can reply. Making content around those inquiries will have an immediate and significant impact on your current clients.

- As a content maker, you ought to consistently know about the subjects your known and anonymous contenders are expounding on in your space. Seeing how your rivals approach a subject will assist you with separating your brand's voice, approach, and content from theirs, recognize holes in their content system, and help your content stand out in the sales process.

- Your association wide information is an integral asset to use when concocting new ideas for your content. For instance, your client assistance group has a ton of understanding into the everyday issues your clients have. Your business group has an abundance of information about which arrangements potential clients need from you or need to hear the most about. Tapping different gatherings in your organization will help distinguish ideas for your content that address your client's needs.

- As an advertiser, your first duty is to comprehend your client. In this way, when you are searching for groundbreaking ideas, consider what your client may discover connecting with, intriguing or supportive. At that point investigate how those thoughts could function with your content procedure. You can look at different websites or social sites to discover what subjects individuals are getting some information about in your specialized topics.

- Research using key words is a fabulous method to find how your crowd is discussing a point. Moreover, keyword examination can assist you with finding open doors for content that you might not have considered before.

Once you have finished the phase of idea creation and know which topic you want to create the content about, the next step is to plan and outline what you are going to create. The initial phase in arranging your bit of content is to choose what shape you need it to take. Some ideas will be stronger if they are represented visually, and could warrant an infographic or video. Other pieces of content may be best suited for plaintext. For those, a blog post, article, or eBook might be the best form. You can gain a lot of insight by investigating which types of content have already been created around your topic.

Furthermore, during all the stages you will need to ensure you are doing suitable key word research around your theme. When making web content you will have to choose a watchword to target with the goal that you can incorporate the key word suitably into your substance as you compose, not afterward. Content creation is always based on strategies. A content strategy includes everything from brand and tone to how you will promote your content and eventually repurpose it.

Content creation is a definitive inbound marketing practice. At the point when you make your content, you are without giving and valuable data to your crowd, pulling in expected clients to your site, and holding existing clients through quality commitment. Content exists all over the place, yet its prosperity depends on your capacity to adjust it to the medium on which it lives. One size does not fit all when it comes to posting on different mediums or the platforms within those mediums, for that matter. Web-based media content fluctuates from blog content, which is unique in relation to site content.

Along these lines, you need to realize how to tailor your creation to contact your crowd where they are. Content creation is an iterative cycle that pays off immensely with your crowd. When you have the substance creation measure down, you will have the option to produce innovative work that amuses your crowd as well as develops your business.

2.1 Content Creation in the Modern Age

For an appropriate depiction of a substance maker, we need to initially characterize content. As you probably are aware, content is just data wrapped up and introduced in a gleaming bundle. That bundle can be physical, for example, the substance inside a book, paper, or magazine or computerized, for example, the substance you will discover on a site, blog, or web-based media stage. Consequently, a content maker is the individual liable for making that data.

In the present computerized world, making content should be a top objective to expand more inbound traffic to your site and become a confided advisor. Start by identifying a handful of employees who could provide quality blog content and then start out at two per month if you are new to blogging. To make sure to stay on top of the craft, block out an hour on your calendar each month to dedicate to writing your post. From there, move to bi-weekly posts and then weekly. Making a consistent content stream does not occur incidentally, yet the more exertion you put in toward it, the more noteworthy your return will be. Over the long haul, your content will turn out to be better made and more instructive, making your site the most visited website for applicable information inside your industry.

Numerous individuals do not understand how indispensable having a routinely refreshed blog can be to natural pursuit rankings. Truth be told, social media today goes far enough to state, there is certifiably not a superior method to add pertinent substance to your site consistently than to use a blog. Adding elegantly composed, instructive content not just urges forthcoming clients to visit your website, it likewise builds the page count for your actual website.

For example, if you compose two online journals in seven days that means two totally new pages are added to your site each week just from the blog. This training normally comes down to procuring connections to content, which significantly helps in website streamlining (SEO). Each time you compose another blog; make certain to add labels, watchwords, and a Meta depiction to streamline the page. In any case, basically composing content just to compose content is not the best strategy. The content should be useful and top notch, making your organization's blog a place of gaining education.

Despite the business, being viewed as an idea chief makes a feeling of trust from current and forthcoming clients. If you are a designing organization gaining practical experience in electrical sources, being a confided in source on everything electric for instance, electric vehicles and the most recent patterns in this space separates your organization from others in the business. This educational content lets your potential consumers know the wealth of knowledge you have on your product and service, creating trust.

The content should be made on purchaser personas and the purchaser's excursion to fabricate trust through established idea initiative. Purchaser personas speak to ideal clients and should be the fundamental concentration for building up your content plan and methodology.

The goal should be to solve your personas' problems through educating them on a topic.

Similarly, the buyer's journey focuses on what stage of the funnel the perspective customer falls under. By catering content to fit the proper stage, it ensures that the buyer feels understood and in capable hands.

In current advertising, you do not just deliver substance and leave it on the site to occupy room but you share it. Web-based media sharing most importantly straightforwardly elevates the substance to your devotees. From that point onward, it goes above and beyond, urging your following to share the post somewhere else. This can likewise urge different distributers to share your substance on their foundation too, for example, a comparable designing firm who discovered your article on electrical switches valuable. Along these lines, your content starts to spread online by having more inbound connections to your webpage, eventually driving up your website authority with Google.

Following distributing another blog entry, you ought to have a mechanized email send it to your bought in email list, telling them new content is accessible and urging them to connect significantly further with you. If social sharing buttons are optimized in the email, they can then easily share the content on social media or forward your email along to a colleague, further promoting your content at no extra cost or effort for you. As the content is shared, your company name and site are also shared across emails, social media, and the Internet, gaining even more credibility and potential visitors that could convert to leads down the road.

You could state that content makers are simply imaginative business people. Yet, it is an entire other calling with an alternate arrangement of rules. Business people earn enough to pay the rent assembling a business. Their item is their organization, their image, and they try to offer some incentive to their objective client.

When you are a content maker, you are a business person as in you work for yourself, and make something from nothing. There are likewise now numerous business visionaries who are content makers too. These two callings go incredible together, as one feeds the other. In the event that you have a drawn in crowd, you can change a portion of that into clients, and the other way around. Although, content makers are above all else, communicators. Their occupation is making content professionally. Also, similarly as there are various business people, working in various enterprises, there are diverse content makers, working in various mediums i.e., video, text, sound, and visual.

The two professions entrepreneurship and content creation are coming together in the days ahead. Back in the twentieth century, you had to choose from either to follow the money or follow your passion. Today, business, art, and profit are linked. They came together in a sense that only content creator people who create for a living can understand. In the always changing advanced world, content creation has gotten more helpful than any other time in recent memory for boosting SEO, building up idea initiative and trust, pulling in guests and producing leads, and advancement and sharing.

2.2 History of Content Marketing

Promoting content pushes us to consistently be searching for better approach to get things done. There are a lot of new strategies out there standing by to be found, yet we can likewise gain from widespread exercises previously instructed. Time is an extraordinary sifter, eliminating from memory what did not work while saving what succeeded. We call the record of those victories and disappointments history.

Just like we can learn from the lessons of recorded history, we can also learn from the successes and failures of early marketing. After all, those strategies transformed some brands into modern household essentials. So, strap in and prepare for a ride through the history of content marketing.

The earliest piece of documented content creation is thought to be John Deere's The Furrow. However, recent research has revealed that Benjamin Franklin might also have been a very early adopter of the trend when he published the yearly Poor Richard's Almanack in 1732 to promote his printing business.

During the 1800s, the idea of making content to advance organizations was grown considerably further when bookstore Librairie Galignani opened an understanding room and a printed paper that exhibited articles from persuasive writers and books at that point. This was one of the more inventive thoughts at that point. Now, the term content creation had never passed through anybody's lips. Also, it was an extensive, troublesome cycle putting something out there for the sole motivation behind inventive advancement.

Most organizations who fiddled with content creation in the good old days made huge, independent bits of substance and delivered them perhaps just a single a year like the Michelin Guide, which was delivered in 1900 and the Jell-O Company's free formula book which was distributed in 1904. It was not until 2001 that the term content advertising had introduced and, in this manner, it is sidekick content creation was first utilized by Penton Custom Media in Ohio appears to be quite a while really taking shape. From that point forward, content creation has detonated into a totally extraordinary monster. It is not, at this point a tremendous experience to make one bit of uber content every year.

Brands make, distribute, and advance content every day rather than yearly. However, maybe the greatest change is the means by which more modest brands and organizations can utilize content creation and showcasing to stand apart among the serious weapons. However, simply having similar dissemination techniques as media organizations is not sufficient if you need to stick out, particularly with the sheer measure of advertisers zeroing in intensely on substance creation. Brands need to get innovative; truly inventive.

When PCs and Internet use started to spread over the world, another channel for content advertising was conceived. Advertisers began investigating ways they could utilize this new, advanced media, from sites to messages and significantly more. In 1993, O'Reilly and Associates was the primary business to dispatch a business site. This was actually the second when content broke the syndication that publicizing had on the media. Anybody with a web association could now make and forward their content.

The expression content promoting was brought into the world in 1996 at a conversation for columnists at the American Society for Newspaper Editors. Little did John F. Oppedahl know when he said the expression that it would immediately get one of the main terms in marketing. In 1994, the main blog was made by Justin Hall of Swarthmore College. While a few websites have consistently been utilized as a sort of advanced journal, sites acquainted the open door for brands with associate with their crowds, share more content, and keep on building their image and tone. Blog turned into a term in 1999 when it was abbreviated from weblog.

The Internet turned into a unique channel, a research center where content advertisers could ceaselessly discover better approaches to associate with crowds. Indeed, so much substance joined the web that in the mid-21st century, positioning calculations must be created to some way or another deal with the tremendous measures of content.

Facebook, initially called Facebook, began in 2003 and remains the channel of decision for purchaser advertisers. In 2006, Twitter joined the informal community club and brands immediately began utilizing it to take part continuously discussions with buyers about items and different issues. YouTube rose in 2005 and made a historic point of reference for recordings in substance promoting.

A considerable lot of the jumps in substance promoting happened on the grounds that brands adjusted to propelling innovation. Brands that did not adjust do not exist today. Second, consistently recollect your crowd. We would not be the place where we are today if brands like Michelin and Jell-O had not begun focusing on explicit gatherings. All of the businesses we have discussed were trying something fresh, and any time a business tries something outside the box, it is risky.

In this advanced period of content showcasing, attempting to advertise your item or administration will just not work. What you ought to do rather is to convey the specific message you need to pass on to your buyers in a certified and legit way. There are many content advertising strategies that you ought to continue to succeed. It does not make a difference who your intended interest group is on the grounds that it is almost certain that they made and external layer as their assurance from the fusillade of messages they manage each and every day. Placing your confidence in your clients will cause them to react in kind.

After you had your first discussion with your crowd, do not simply hand your business card over and proceed onward to the following possibility. All connections expect time to create and the sort of relationship you need to shape with your crowd is not exclusion.

Thus, do not mull over investing some exertion and energy in becoming acquainted with your crowd in the most ideal manner you can.

This is essentially clear as crystal and is in reality significant taking everything into account. You could never need your crowd to feel as though you are not at all ready to build up a relationship with them. Rather than pushing each other away, you just as your crowd can frame and support a strong and solid relationship. Find that availability and offer your crowd with the opportunity to give a positive reaction to your message.

2.3 Importance of Content Marketing

Content advertising is a promoting cycle that acknowledges a lot the way that most customers are presently prepared to do totally dismissing the commotion of the marketing efforts they are being presented to consistently. It is a method that includes making and curating extraordinary, pertinent content that your clients will discover helpful and significant. It is the craft of speaking with your likely clients without straightforwardly offering to them.

Rather than just selling your administrations and items, you are offering data to your planned clients that can show them something. Whenever done accurately, you will advertise without intruding on your clients' lives and you could at last be remunerated with their business, loyalty and support.

Content promoting is utilized to draw in and build up a particular objective crowd with a definitive objective of making genuine client commitment. Through utilizing content promotion, you should endeavor to change and upgrade your client's conduct toward your organization in a positive way. If you reliably convey important data to your clients you will have the option to pick up their trust and following. Following are some reasons why content marketing is essential:

- It helps your SEO, since web indexes reward organizations that distribute exceptional, quality content.

- It makes content which drives inbound traffic and leads.

- It centers around possessing media instead of just getting it.

- It is a fruitful PR methodology. It lets you address issues clients care about instead of simply advancing your business.

- It improves your web-based media methodology.

The basic part of content marketing becomes an integral factor with expanding the volume of value traffic to your site, creating mindfulness, quality leads and deals. Planned and appropriately executed content has the ability to pull your crowd to your business' site, which is at last where they will change over into leads, and afterward deals. The best method to direct people to your site is through the content that you create for your blog, for SEO and for your web-based media promoting. While there are a lot of significant components that live under these classes, everything reduces to the nature of your content.

Basically, content advertising is rapidly turning into the way to having a fruitful promoting effort for your business. Faithful clients are basic to the accomplishment of your business. You should dial in your content marketing methodology, and fuse incredible content and bits of knowledge that your current client's esteem. At that point you will exploit the intensity of custom content to reinforce these significant client connections.

Building up your online content should fill different needs. For instance, it ought to incorporate content that will pull in success in your business, and will keep clients engaged in with incredible content developed explicitly for post-buy utilization. Content that offers some incentive for your client base will help increment brand steadfastness by fortifying those connections you have with your clients on the web. This serves to encourage repeat sales with cross-selling and up-selling opportunities.

Extraordinary content can keep going for an everlastingly time on the internet, proceeding to convey indexed lists and advantages for a long time to come. You just need to see the dates of content that surface in an inquiry to see that the best content ages smoothly on the web. Therefore, the content you produce which positions well will move in the rankings over the long run, bringing continuous upgrades to your websites. Incredible content which different destinations connect to can produce long haul traffic lifts to your site with sound degrees of natural traffic or new qualified site guests. In the present business world, grandstand yourself as a valid and dependable provider through good content. Accordingly, your digital marketing strategy, and specifically the quality of your content, will attract and convert new customers to your business.

2.4 Managing the Content Creation Process

Content creation is actually what it seems like i.e., it is the way toward making and executing on moving and applicable points through the privilege computerized source or item. As such, you need an informed content showcasing group that is loaded with dedicated authors who comprehend the value that watchwords, publication schedules and web-based media bring to incredible content.

The way in to your prosperity is finding a cycle that works for you. A working content creation measure is basic if you need to accomplish your center showcasing objectives, which are likely:

- Instructing readers.
- Directing people to your site.
- Catching leads.
- Improving on the web perceivability.
- Drawing in with your social following.
- Picking up validity.
- Building brand mindfulness.

Customers have no interest in processing ads they are compelled to peruse i.e., 66 percent of individuals skip TV ad promotions and 44 percent disregard direct messages. Notwithstanding, 70% of individuals conceded that they would prefer to find out about an item or administration offered by an organization through an article rather than a conventional promotion. Following is a step-by-step guide to developing your own effective content creation process, plus some helpful tools and resources to manage your content creation process:

1. Before you can produce compelling content, you need to consider why you are doing it in any case. Think about the accompanying inquiries when building up your content objectives:

- Is it accurate to say that you are resolved to carry clear attention to your image?

- Would you like to direct people to a specific segment of your site?

- Would you like to instruct your readers and become an idea chief?

- Have you considered content as a method for pushing readers through the business channel?

- What sort of content is at present moving/how would you like to utilize this data during your own inventive cycle?

2. Did you choose to re-appropriate your content promoting endeavors, or would you say you are employing an in-house group to streamline your site for the New Year? All colleagues i.e., SEO specialists, planners, videographers, venture supervisors, journalists, editors, fashioners, and so forth ought to comprehend your center objectives prior to making content, so incorporate them during the underlying conversation of what you need to escape the content. It is anything but an impractical notion to reassign colleagues to various tasks toward the start of the year only if you need to give your content a new point of view.

3. By knowing precisely who your intended interest group is, you can create customized content that is effortlessly delighted in and processed, grow long haul associations with readers and even increment brand mindfulness over the long haul. During your

examination cycle, figure out what your crowd needs constantly dependent on the items and administrations you offer. From that point, you can begin the arranging and ideation measure.

4. Now, an exact and achievable course of events should be examined and an article schedule should be made. This is an ideal opportunity to dole out items dependent on each colleague's strength. Try not to leave this underlying gathering alone the main time the group gets together. A week after week or fortnightly gathering, or even a basic email string that is returned to consistently, can keep everybody associated and forestall any interruptions in the inventive cycle.

5. The exploration cycle will appropriately set you up for conceptualizing and ideation. During this stage, consider your crowd and your objectives as content makers and how you can appropriately associate with your readers. Examination moving points that are pertinent to your industry so you do not go into your meeting to generate new ideas dumbfounded. While the person who is making each bit of content will do the majority of the exploration dependent on their own venture, it is anything but a poorly conceived notion to include other colleagues who can contribute. For instance, an online media tactician can assist an author with understanding what is moving continuously, and can share such data during the conceptualizing cycle.

6. Once you get a sense of trending topics, as well as which keywords you need to target, it is time to start brainstorming and developing solid ideas that will work best for your brand in terms of content strategy. This is a great time to get a sense of how your content creation team works each member may have a different strategy for ideation. For instance, authors may take the good old course and get a stack of paper and let the pen

coast until they are confused, utilizing their own insight to think of thoughts and adding catchphrases when they are done. Different makers may allude to the watchwords and make an advanced flowchart dependent on the research.

7. If your creators have a difficult time coming up with ideas on their own, think about having a meeting for brainstorming and collaboration. You can develop a wide variety of large-scale topics, and then have each individual team member develop his or her own shorter, more detailed topics based on the type of content he or she is creating, whether it's a blog post, infographic or video.

8. Try not to let the entirety of this new substance you made for the New Year sit on a rack. Over the long haul, your content will age, however that does not mean it is transformed into something pointless. Streamline your substance to make it more appealing, helpful and significant to your intended interest group. Experiencing another round of catchphrase research and executing new terms where they fit in the duplicate is a straightforward and viable approach to make your content applicable once more.

With your showcasing schedule and content creation plan close by, it is an ideal opportunity to add some supplemental content. All things considered, publishing one blog a month will not get you far if your rivals are posting two, three, four, or more occasions each month. The supplemental content could be articles, recordings, or sounds. It very well may be editorial of recent developments or another article you read, or a recap or audit of an instrument or asset you found.

To start with, pick two bits of supplemental content to add to your advertising schedule for every month. Consider choosing one quick easy post type and one more involved, like an article and a review, or an article and a commentary piece. Second, reach out to podcast hosts, radio shows, event hosts, and entrepreneurs who host tele classes and webinars about being a guest. Set an objective to do one meeting or talking commitment every month, at that point compose a blog promoting it.

Content creation is not just about long-structure articles. It can mean video, sound, articles, interviews, infographics, slide decks, analysis, surveys, and then some. Stirring up the sort of content you share makes it simple to share all the more regularly and makes it more diversion for your crowd to draw in with your content, as well. Zero in on making content that will not just have a quick effect in your business, your frameworks and measures, and your productivity, yet additionally your promoting and master situating. Focus on your promoting schedule and content creation plan, ensuring it is attainable and sensible. Likewise, if you do not do that you are falling behind your objectives, getting baffled, feeling overpowered, and deserting it.

Remain steady in your efforts. Once more, content creation is a long-distance race not a run. By chance that you need assistance, do not be hesitant to request it. With regards to content creation, it is anything but difficult to begin and stop, to get inspired, compose a pack, at that point get going and distribute nothing for quite a long time or months all at once. Making a feasible content creation measure that you can adhere to over the long run is more diligently. It requires work and exertion, yet the awards far surpass the exertion. Keep in mind that if content creation was simple, everybody would do it. All you require to stress over it more than your rivals.

Chapter 3: Converting Personal Social Media to Business Social Media

In case you are similar to most Americans, or possibly most experts, you are as of now fairly active via online media. You likely have individual records on Facebook, Twitter, LinkedIn and Instagram, in addition to associations and supporters on each application. Also, you presumably incidentally post substance that keeps you pretty much drew in with those crowds.

Truth be told, you are now posting what an undeniable online media showcasing effort would post. The main contrasts are heading, goal and scale. Anyway, consider the possibility that you fired scaling-up your own efforts. Imagine a scenario where you aggregated a crowd of people of thousands, many thousands, possibly countless supporters at that point transformed those reasonable online media endeavors into an undeniable business that made you cash.

To be sure, online media is perhaps the most ideal approaches to interface with individuals who as of now love your brand. It is likewise significant for arriving at the individuals who have not known about your business yet. Not all things can be a business. It you need to make a benefit; you need to offer something significant. Something else, nearly anybody can begin a business regardless of whether that implies proficient administrations, such as counseling or autonomous provisional labor. Thus, do some conceptualizing before you endeavor the real change measure; you will need a reasonable strategy before you continue. Following are the general steps you need to follow:

1. **Create a Plan**

Social instruments are anything but difficult to utilize and you can begin with natural posts for nothing.

That may make it enticing to make a plunge and simply begin posting. Yet, similar to each great business system, utilizing online media for independent venture achievement needs to begin with a decent plan. Without a plan, you have no unmistakable objective for what you are attempting to accomplish. That implies it is extremely unlikely to gauge your outcomes. Do the effort to make an online media plan right in the beginning. This guarantees that all your social endeavors uphold explicit business objectives.

2. Learn about your Target Audience

One explanation utilizing online media for business is so successful is that you can know your crowd. Above all, you need to comprehend who your crowd is. Start by arranging information on your present clients. At that point, burrow further with online media examination. You will begin to build up a strong image of who is purchasing from you and connecting with you on the web.

3. Learn which Platforms are right for you

Try not to make suppositions about where your crowd invests their energy on the web. Your sense may disclose to you that in case you are focusing on recent college grads, you should skip Facebook and spotlight on Instagram and Snapchat. Yet, the information shows that 84% of recent college grads actually use Facebook.

4. Expand your Target Audience

When you have an idea about who your crowd is, you can return to your web-based media plan. It is an ideal opportunity to search for approaches to contact more individuals simply like them.

You can likewise utilize online media to drive new clients to your nearby business. For instance, search streams can help you screen and react to nearby discussions about your business and assemble associations with other neighborhood organizations in your general vicinity.

5. Build Relationships

The remarkable advantage of online media for private venture is that it permits you to talk straightforwardly to clients and supporters. You can fabricate connections after some time. Over 40% of computerized buyers utilize informal communities to investigate new brands or items. A piece of that disclosure is becoming acquainted with who you are as a brand.

When people engage with your organic content or ads, it is a great idea to engage back. This assists with building trust and structure over a period. As fans offer and like your content, you ascend in the social calculations and gain new and free exposure. You likewise support connections that can turn into deals in the times ahead. You can likewise assemble associations with different business people and influencers in your specialty. Think your business is too little to even consider working with influencers? Small influencers can be successful for building up brand trust. As a little something extra, they are regularly well inside the spending scope of many brands.

6. Share visuals on your Social Media

People have come to expect social posts to include a visual component. In the event that your content does not look great, nobody will quit looking to read what you need to state. Yet, even tweets benefit from a good graphic. For administration organizations specifically, extraordinary symbolism can be somewhat of a test.

However, each business can recount its story through photographs and recordings. Possibly you can exhibit your organization culture with pictures from inside your office. Another choice is to utilize stock photographs. There are a lot of free, top notch photographs online that you can use in your social posts. Or on the other hand possibly you can utilize photographs of your clients to feature how they utilize your administration.

7. Focus on Quality rather than Quantity

The sheer number of web-based media promoting choices for private venture may appear to be overpowering yet you do not have to do it all. It is more imperative to make quality content on a few key channels than it is to have a presence on each and every application. Most importantly, be certain that your social posts offer worth. By chance that everything you do is pitch and sell, there is almost no inspiration for individuals to follow you. Keep in mind, social advertising is tied in with building connections. Be human. Be straightforward. Post incredible content.

8. Track and refine your Social Media Posts

As you actualize your social technique, it is imperative to monitor what works and what does not. You would then be able to calibrate your efforts and improve results. The investigation devices referenced above give you an extraordinary image of your social efforts and can help track whichever measurements matter most to you. When you have a thought of how your technique is functioning, it is an ideal opportunity to begin searching for approaches to improve.

Regardless of the size of your business, social apparatuses can help you associate in a better way with your crowd, arrive at new likely clients, and increment attention to your image. On the off chance that the conceivable outcomes appear to be overpowering, start little.

Keep in mind you do not have to do it all. Adopt an engaged strategy. Start with a couple of key efforts and assemble your online media promoting endeavors over the long run.

Your direction should be continually pushing ahead in the web-based media world. Draw in with more elevated level influencers. Get distributed on greater, higher-traffic distributers. Continue drawing in with new crowds to extend your followings. The more you participate in these developmental efforts, the more definitive and amazing you will become, and both your client following and maintenance will improve.

Your web-based media crowd, whenever tapped to its maximum capacity, can give you a monstrous head start regarding client procurement, however it is actually up to you to deliver the best-in-class products and services that your audience will have come to expect from you. Be a business person first, and a web-based media master second; that is the main way you will endure. Building a business is not easy, no matter what kind of runway you build for yourself or what mediums you enlist to help you along the way. Be prepared for this eventuality.

3.1 Setting up Your Social Media Account

Setting up a social media account requires have a strategy so that you can eventually succeed. A social media strategy is a summary of everything you plan to do and hope to achieve on social media. It guides your actions and lets you know whether you are succeeding or failing. The more specific your plan is, the more effective it will be. Keep it concise. Do not make it so lofty and broad that it is unattainable or impossible to measure. Following are some steps to follow:

1. Pick online media advertising objectives that adjust to your business goals

The initial step to making a triumphant system is to build up your destinations and objectives. Without objectives, you have no real way to gauge achievement and degree of profitability (ROI). Every one of your objectives should be:

- Specific

- Measurable

- Attainable

- Relevant

- Time-bound

This is the S.M.A.R.T. objective structure. It will control your activities and guarantee they lead to genuine business results. Vanity measurements like number of adherents and preferences are anything but difficult to follow, however it is difficult to demonstrate their genuine worth. All things considered, center around things like commitment, navigation, and transformation rates. You might need to follow various objectives for various applications, or even various uses for each application.

For instance, if by chance you use LinkedIn to direct people to your site, you would quantify click-through. In the event that Instagram is for the awareness of your brand, you may follow the quantity of views in your Instagram Story. In the event that you promote on Facebook, cost-per-click (CPC) is a typical achievement metric. Online media objectives ought to line up with your general showcasing targets. This makes it simpler to show the estimation of your work and secure purchase in from your chief. Begin building up your online media advertising plan by writing down three objectives for web-based media.

2. Learn everything about your clients

One of the worst mistakes to make on social media is coming off as the faceless corporation with zero personality. In the modern age of transparency, people want to get to know your company on a more personal level. Many brands today crack jokes and are not afraid to talk to their followers like they would their friends.

Whereas brands were once lambasted for coming off like robots, a human social media presence has become an expectation among many followers. Knowing who your audience is and what they want to see on social media is the key. That way you can create content that they will like, comment on, and share. It is also critical if you want to turn social media followers into customers for your business. Get to know your fans, followers, and customers as real people with real wants and needs, and you will know how to target and engage them on social media. When it comes to your target customer, you should know things like:

- Age
- Location
- average income
- Typical job title or industry
- Interests

3. Create editorial alerts for your account

If there is a common thread between the biggest brands on social, it is that they post on a consistent basis. Chances are you are juggling multiple social channels and are trying to make sure you tick a lot of boxes in terms of descriptions and when to post. Consider how a content calendar can make the process much easier by:

- Timing your presents on amplify commitment, shielding you from having to continually post continuously.

- Try not to rehash a similar content again and again; guaranteeing every one of your articles or pictures gets the most love conceivable.

- Make a timetable carries out double responsibility of keeping your web-based media presence coordinated while additionally amplifying your content's span.

4. Automate the right way

Automation is extremely popular in advertising at this moment, and in light of current circumstances. Nonetheless, you cannot hope to effectively put your social presence on autopilot and leave. Quick forward to introduce day and unmistakably client care is a bit of web-based media that should be customized, not mechanized. Automation through planning or curating content is thoroughly reasonable game. Simply evade it when you are managing genuine clients or followers inquiries. This is the reason brands depend on social devices to help clergyman bits of substance previously affirmed by showcasing pioneers.

5. Know your competition before you enter the world of social media

Odds are your competitors are already using social media, and that means you can learn from what they are doing. A competitive analysis allows you to understand who the competition is and what they are doing well. You will get a good sense of what is expected in your industry, which will help you set social media targets of your own. It will also help you spot opportunities.

Possibly one of your rivals is prevailing on Facebook, for instance, yet has invested little energy into Twitter or Instagram. You should zero in on the organizations where your crowd is underserved, as opposed to attempting to win fans from a predominant player.

Social listening is another approach to watch out for your rivals. Do searches of the opposition's organization name, account handles, and other significant catchphrases via online media. Discover what they are sharing and what others are stating about them.

6. Make an amazing profile

As you decide which social networks to use, you will also need to define your strategy for each. Once you have decided which networks to focus on, it is time to create your profiles. Or improve existing ones so they align with your strategy.

- Use consistent branding (logos, images, etc.) across networks so your profiles are easily recognizable
- Include keywords people would use to search for your business
- Make sure you fill out all profile fields

7. Find your inspiration

While it is significant that your brand be special, you can in any case draw motivation from different organizations that are extraordinary on social. You can generally locate these on the business segment of the informal community's site. Contextual investigations can offer important bits of knowledge that you can apply to your own online media plan.

Who do you appreciate following via online media? What do they do that forces individuals to connect with and share their content? Notice that every one of these records has a predictable voice, tone, and style.

That is vital to telling individuals what is in store from your feed. That is, the reason would it be advisable for them to follow you? How might this benefit them? Consistency additionally helps keep your content on-brand regardless of whether you have different individuals on your web-based media group.

Shoppers can likewise offer online media motivation. What are your objective clients discussing on the web? What would you be able to find out about their needs constantly? In the event that you have existing social channels, you could likewise ask your supporters what they need from you. Simply ensure that you finish and deliver what they request.

Online media moves quick. New organizations arise, others experience segment shifts. Your business will experience times of progress too. The entirety of this implies that your web-based media methodology should be a living report that you audit and change varying. Allude to it regularly to remain on target; however, do not be hesitant to improve changes with the goal that it reflects new objectives, apparatuses, or plans.

Overviews can likewise be an incredible method to discover how well your procedure is functioning. Ask your supporters, email list, and site guests whether you are living up to their requirements and desires, and what they would prefer. At that point try to convey on what they let you know. When you update your social media, try to tell everybody in your group. That way they would all be able to cooperate to help your business capitalize on your records.

3.2 Establish the Best Social Media Posts

Online media achievement requires solid composing aptitudes. Although, not all web-based media chiefs see themselves as essay writers. Luckily, composing incredible online media content does not need to be troublesome. Not every post needs to reinvent the copywriting wheel, after all. All things considered, doing the effort to get your composing right is justified, despite any trouble. Each social post you add depicts about your brand. In case you are messy, your organization will look messy as well. Surprisingly the most dreadful point is that it could sabotage your prosperity via online media.

That is the reason it is imperative to compose well via web-based media. Online media copywriting requires some extraordinary aptitudes. You should have the option to pack however using a couple of words as could reasonably be expected. You additionally must be steady and connecting consistently. Furthermore, every application is one of a kind. What chips away at Facebook may slump on LinkedIn. This makes turning into an expert social scribe much more troublesome

Advertisers are relied upon to shuffle numerous social profiles and stay up with the latest new posts. It is a very intense job. Your supporters are ravenous for new content and you are relied upon to convey consistently. However, when you continually reuse similar posts over and over, your social feeds begin to feel like a burial ground. That is actually why brands need to have different web-based media ideas in their back pocket. Following are some amazing techniques that you can use to generate amazing posts for your social media accounts:

1. Create a Daily, Weekly or Monthly Series

Need to cause your social feed to feel more like an occasion versus a clothing rundown of irregular posts? Start an arrangement where you have the occasion to communicate with your fans and devotees consistently. Speaking with devotees by means of Twitter is easy and just requires a marked hashtag to begin. By consistently planning these meetings, supporters can leave their voices alone heard while additionally captivating with your brand.

Picking the minds of your adherents shows that you care about them, yet in addition encourages you to tap into your crowd's torments and concerns. If you are struggling to show up to your social feeds, a regular series is a solid starting point.

2. Organize a Giveaway or Contest

Individuals cannot avoid the intensity of anything given for free. Running an intermittent challenge is one of the most effective online media thoughts with regards to likely commitment from supporters. As indicated by information from Tailwind, 91% of Instagram posts with in excess of 1,000 likes or remarks are identified with a challenge. In the interim, accounts that run challenges consistently are noted to become 70% quicker than those that did not. You do not really require an outside arrangement or administration to run a challenge. All you require is a mix of the accompanying points:

- In a perfect world, the prize for your challenge should by one way or another be identified with your brand. Expensive, inconsequential things will in general draw in gift searchers that will not convert into long haul adherents.

- To cover yourself lawfully, terms and conditions are an absolute necessity for your challenge.

- On your footing and conditions page, make a point to leave an email address where individuals can connect with questions or concerns.

- Regardless of whether it is through client created content or a hashtag, getting some information about your brand is the most ideal approach to empower passages. All things considered, the motivation behind a giveaway is brand mindfulness, not simply to part with free stuff.

Hashtags are by a wide margin the easiest methods for monitoring who participated in your challenge for nothing. You do not have to pursue challenges weekly to receive the benefits. Challenges are an incredible method to spike your devotee check and commitment, and are an extraordinary online media thought for crusades you are hoping to upgrade, for example, new item launches.

3. Host an AMA

An AMA (ask me anything) arrangement speaks to a marvelous occasion to teach and draw in with your adherents. AMA's are basically Q&A meetings where you will share your insight, encounters and understanding. If you have conquered battles or have clout in your industry, you probably have the cleaves to lead an AMA. From sharing examples of overcoming adversity to individual difficulties, such meetings can be convincing for crowds and brands the same.

You will flaunt your own side, displaying the face in the background of your business. You bring issues to light for your image without being pushy or salesy about it. You study the worries and interests of your crowd. If you have an enormous group, you can urge every part to lead their own AMA after some time to give such a higher perspective on your brand.

4. Organize a Social Media Takeover

At times infusing some new life into your social feeds implies letting another person dominate. Takeovers put the reigns of your social records in another person's hands, generally for a time of 24 hours. Giving off your social presence to an influencer or big name with a huge, dynamic crowd is a prime method to get your brand before some new faces, just as infuse another voice into your record if you feel you are running low via online media post ideas. You can likewise let another person in your application assume control over your record to give your feed some flavor.

Consider colleagues and industry connections that could be acceptable possibility for a takeover. The motivation behind a takeover is to get introduction, so in a perfect world pick somebody who's crowd segment is pertinent to your own.

5. Share your Posts

Try not to be hesitant to let your fans and supporters do the talking. Keep in mind, not the entirety of the content on your social feed must be your own. Indeed, standard way of thinking discloses to us that it should not be. Advancing other pertinent brands, articles and photographs from your devotees is an extraordinary content thought that shows that you are important for your industry's discussion, not simply a parrot. Your feeds should be comprised of 80% engaging constantly content and just 20% special content. This shields your feed from feeling like an attempt to sell something.

In the case of nothing else, a Regram or Retweet is generally easy. Not all online media present thoughts have on be top to bottom or muddled, particularly in the event that you as of now have a devoted following.

6. Bite Size Video Clips

Video content showcasing has become an unquestionable requirement accomplish for present day brands. Unfortunately, many see the investment in video as being too complicated or out of their reach. But when you consider that video content gets exponentially more shares than video or text, brands should give some serious thought to creative social media ideas that incorporate video.

That is the reason scaled down video cuts is as yet an ideal thought for Twitter, Instagram and Facebook. Such clasps require negligible altering, can be shot very quickly and are prime for sharing. Try not to stress recording out and out plugs, but instead short, inventive clasps to keep your devotees engaged.

7. Repurpose your Content

Think about the planning, effort and sheer amount of time it takes to create any piece of content. Does it not bode well to crush as much as possible out each blog entry or video you make? For each blog entry you compose or video you shoot, you ought to consider extra thoughts for advancing it via web-based media past its unique configuration.

Presently, suppose you repurposed each blog entry you composed or video you shared. You would have a very decent overabundance of sharable content. Repurposing your content not just inhales new life into old or in any case disregarded posts, yet in addition shields your adherents from getting exhausted of a similar message shared again and again.

8. Team Up with Another Brand

Co-marketing is a win-win situation. Two brands collaborate on a mission or bit of content, for example, an online course, digital book or even an extraordinary promotion. Each company gets presentation to the next crowd.

Online media is the ideal stage for co-advertising effort thoughts since it is so natural to match up your endeavors. Search for brands to join forces with that are not contenders yet have a comparative objective crowd.

3.3 Start Gaining Profit from Your Social Media Account

Many experts say that social media is for connecting with people, and not for selling, but at some point, you are going to want to leverage the connections you create. If you have built up enough trust with your followers, they will be more inclined to check out your recommendations and the links you share. Following are the techniques you can use to start earning on social media:

1. Create and Promote Your Own Information Products

If you as of now have a blog, and you have exhibited your ability on a particular subject throughout some stretch of time, there might be an occasion to make a digital book, sound program or video course and offer it to your crowd. Web-based media is the ideal spot to advance such an item. Similarly, as with anything, quality is vital to making something individuals need to peruse, however will pay to peruse. By chance that you take additional consideration in making incredible data, planning and advancing it well, you will get more sales.

2. Use Visual Media to Promote Crafts

If you will in general make handcrafted makes, craftsmanship pieces, or even pieces of clothing and weaving, there might be an occasion to grandstand your items via web-based media.

Instagram and Pinterest may seem like evident spots to hit, yet Facebook, Twitter and Google+ are likewise incredible channels for sharing visual media. You can guide your devotees to look at your items there, and between the various channels, you can possibly earn enough to pay the bills.

3. Join the YouTube Partner Program

Building a famous YouTube channel can be a great deal of work. In any case, if you as of now have a following, or you are resolved to assemble your crowd, joining the YouTube Partner Program to bring in cash on promoting may be a way worth investigating. There are noticeable YouTube content makers who have made considerable measures of cash with this program; however, they are the exemption as opposed to the standard. It would require some investment, technique and sheer karma to bring in cash on YouTube. However, this is a good thing to keep in mind with advertising in general. Unless you are already getting a lot of views and clicks, you are not going to make a lot of money on them.

4. Promote your Coaching or Consulting Services

Online media is an incredible spot to create leads for your counseling business. Regardless of whether you are a guitar instructor or a holistic mentor, on the off chance that you have exhibited mastery in a particular zone, you can create more interest for your administrations by interfacing with your objective client via online media.

Instructing meetings can be led over Skype, so this is certainly an occasion to bring in cash without venturing out from home. Counseling can be rewarding, so always remember not to undermine yourself charge a reasonable cost for your time and exertion. This system can likewise work as one with selling data items, as the individuals who need your recommendation are bound to be keen to know all the details on the digital books and courses you have made.

5. Promote Products and Services

There are numerous open doors for you to share supported posts that advance the items and administrations of different businesses. This is an immediate method of bringing in cash from online media. In any case, on the off chance that you do not have a sizable following, this may not be a lot of a chance. You likewise need to be careful with over-advancing items for need of cash, since, in such a case that your supporters see that you are continually tweeting around some item, not exclusively will they not snap on the connections, they will likewise un-follow you.

It is essential to blend things up. It is savvy to require some investment to create an appropriate web-based media posting plan, to ensure you are enhancing your adherents while advancing items. Invitations to take action should be a piece of your web-based media technique, yet every post cannot be a source of inspiration.

6. Promote Affiliate Products

Regardless of what industry you are in, you can discover extraordinary items to promote through your social media. However, if that does not exactly jive with you, you can likewise turn into an Amazon Associate, advance results based on your personal preference and procure commissions on them, Amazon has no lack of items. Next, rather than spamming links on Twitter and seeking after the best, remember that the most fair and viable method of advancing member items is through surveys.

If you actually utilize an item and like it, and realize that your devotees serve to profit by it, at that point compose a long-structure survey on your blog, and offer why you like the item. Try not to be hesitant to discuss what you like and do not care about it. You can even utilize a video if that is more your style. Additionally, try to uncover your partner connections.

This is a legitimate necessity in many cases, but on the other hand it is a good practice. Your viewers or readers will value your trustworthiness.

Bringing in cash has never been this simple. The open door that we need to sit from home and pull a benefit is noteworthy. The Internet has ensured it. It will require some investment and work for your business to meet up. The procedures talked about above are only the start. Execute them, and you will have a make way forward. The best part is, you need not bother with a site. You can totally place your idea on your online media channels. It is cheap and simple to get under way. The precarious part is staying dedicated to scaling your business. Start acting on the steps, and you will have a steady stage for your business to take off.

Chapter 4: Social Media Branding

Online media is ending up being one of the most useful assets to advertise your brand and stand apart of the group. At the point when online media marking is done accurately, it can and will assist you with interfacing your objective market in an ideal manner. Online media marking structures a characteristic yet a basic piece of your general showcasing efforts on significant social stages, for example, Facebook, Twitter and LinkedIn.

Online media marking is about reliably utilizing the correct techniques to draw in with your intended interest group via web-based media stages. The point or reason for existing is to help brand awareness. By utilizing the intensity of web-based media branding, you can fabricate a powerful organization of fans who are faithful to your brand as well as anxious to purchase from you.

Branding is a significant stage for any business that needs to produce long haul business. It is tied in with characterizing a big motivator for you and simultaneously pull in possibilities that are probably going to transform into clients. In the underlying branding stages, each business lead is significant, which is the reason it is important to begin the relationship on the correct note.

Web-based media marking makes it simple for you to get more significant individuals into your business channel by giving them motivation to confide in you. At the point when you get social marking right, the remainder of the business cycle turns out to be more effective. Directly from brand presentation to client maintenance, you get results, yet quantifiable outcomes. This means better business and more grounded client connections. There are four key territories that you need to deal with to improve your online media branding game:

1. Your Audience

A major piece of online media marking is understanding and knowing your intended interest group like the rear of your hand. This permits you to take an exact, custom-made methodology with your showcasing efforts. If you want to help your audience, you need to get into their shoes. And look at their problems, wants and needs from their eyes. Ask yourself the right questions to identify them. For instance, what age group does your audience belong to?

2. Your Identity

In request to discover accomplishment with web-based media marking, you need to know your business. What defines your brand personality and how can it separate from the others? What does it look to accomplish? Who and how can it need to dazzle? The clearer you are about your brand character, the simpler it will be to make the correct message.

3. Your Content

Share via online media shapes your image, which is the reason it is necessary that you share the correct kind. The content you share has the power to make or break your social media marketing campaign. So, sharing the proper online media posts on each application ought not to be disregarded.

The intensity of video promoting in web-based media is something advertisers should not dismiss as the traffic from this content is relied upon to ascend to 82% in 2022. Despite the fact that is a decent rate for possible purchasers; remember that the quantity of contenders is additionally developing, particularly on YouTube channels. Indeed, that is the inescapable truth of online media development. Furthermore, since insights express that you just have two seconds to catch a possible purchaser's consideration, you would do well to make a solid video content that would prevent the clients from looking past your video post.

4. Your Design

Visual components, for example, shading palette, typography and so forth assume an urgent part in how your devotees see your brand via online media, which is the reason adjusting your brand plan with your advanced showcasing system is a stage you cannot stand to overlook. Keep in mind, our cerebrums will in general handle visual content 60,000x quicker when contrasted with standard content. It helps you build your brand recognition more.

Online Media Branding Myths to Avoid

Being a business, it is significant that you center around getting great outcomes from your web-based media promoting efforts. Also, for that to occur, you need to guarantee that you are not taking a look at online media promoting from some unacceptable focal point. In other words, you should avoid believing in the following three common myths in order to get positive returns.

A great deal of online media advertisers is centered around getting their content to become a web sensation via web-based media and get whatever number votes or likes as would be prudent. Now, regardless of how you see social media branding, it's simply not possible in real life to get hundreds of thousands of genuine followers in a few weeks on your Instagram account. Nor can you get an unrealistic number of likes or shares in a few days on your Facebook page. Even if you do manage to make it happen, it is not going to be ethical. You will end up interacting with the wrong people. And along the process will hurt your brand image.

Attempt and fabricate a genuine connection with your intended interest group by utilizing online media as an instrument.

Try not to consider getting speedy outcomes. Or maybe, know and comprehend what is most important to your brand. Taking the without rushing or the more patient methodology will make your brand look more dependable over the long run.

You can also choose the showcase the benefits or advantages of your company offerings in your profile description area. Regardless of what business you are in, you should realize that shoppers are more intrigued by your brand's character. While there is no uncertainty that you should attempt to offer the most ideal item, that should not come at the expense of creating and nurturing a positive relationship with your customers. Web-based media is a demonstrated instrument that takes this relationship to the following level. It is how many big and small brands are connecting to consumers, including your competitors.

4.1 Choosing the Best Social Media Platform for your Content

There is not, at this point any inquiry that web-based media is an important advertising apparatus for each business that needs to stay applicable and obvious in the present occupied online world. 92 percent of advertisers state that online media has helped increment presentation, which implies that you are not utilizing web-based media to its fullest; you are passing up an enormous chance.

However, beginning can be troublesome, and in any event, something as apparently straightforward as picking a social stage can be more convoluted than you would suspect. There are a huge number of interpersonal organizations out there to look over, however fortunately you can begin by narrowing it down to the most well known and most generally utilized stages.

From that point, it is tied in with figuring out which stage will give you the presentation you are searching for with the correct crowd, and sorting out which one will help you meet your marketing targets.

Start by Defining Your Goals

There are numerous advantages to utilizing web-based media, yet it is essential to have explicit objectives before you push ahead. For one, your destinations will help decide the social stage you pick, yet in addition the content you make, the crowd you target, and that is only the tip of the iceberg. Here are the absolute most regular advantages of utilizing web-based media that you should focus on:

- Contacting new crowds and new socioeconomics who may be open to your items or administrations.

- Increasing brand awareness and presenting your business to new individuals.

- Finding out about the requirements, needs, and propensities for your crowd and clients.

- Expanding traffic to your site and boosting deals.

- Improving your client care contributions by giving another stage on which clients can connect with grievances, questions, and concerns identifying new leads and prospects that are like your best clients.

Narrowing Down Your Choices

There are web-based media stages out there for everything and everybody, including ones to interface individuals with shared interests, comparable pastimes, equivalent socioeconomics, and considerably more.

The fact of the matter is that there are an excessive number of interpersonal interaction locales out there to actually have a presence on them all, and your time would be better spent focusing on the destinations that get the most traffic. Of all the online media destinations out there, the best ones regarding month-to-month dynamic clients incorporate Facebook, Twitter, Instagram, LinkedIn, and Pinterest.

Determine What Channels Your Audience Is Already Using

The whole purpose of online media advertising is to place you in contact with your best crowd, so it is not prudent to pick a stage where your crowd does not work. Tragically, there is no field of dreams opportunity here where your possibilities will begin to utilize your preferred social foundation since you have made a profile. All things being equal, it is a vastly improved plan to investigate which stages your crowd likes and to search them out on the organizations they are now utilizing.

There are a couple of various ways you can approach finding where your crowd is hanging out on the web, and one of the most direct is a basic client study. Pose inquiries like what social destinations they use, where they get their data on the web, and which influencers they tune in to. Another approach to get data about your crowd is through the online media destinations themselves. With stages like Facebook, you can really inform Facebook regarding your optimal clients, and they will assess the crowd size for you.

Look at the Type of Content You Typically Create

Various sorts of content work better with certain web-based media stages, so it is necessary that you consider the kind of content you like to make and that works best with your brand. Instagram, for example, is about the photos, so it may not be the correct decision if the majority of what you make is long-structure literary content like whitepapers.

The kind of content you make will rely upon various things, including your industry, your brand, and your intended interest group, yet content sorts you may focus on include:

- User-generated content
- Blog posts
- Videos
- Testimonials
- Podcasts
- Webinars and livestreams
- Whitepapers
- Photographs
- eBooks

Pair Your Goals, Audience, and Content with the Right Platform

Whenever you have chosen the objectives you need to accomplish with web-based media, figured out where your crowd is hanging out and chosen what sort of content turns out best for you, you would then be able to experience and contrast the distinctive web-based media stages and figure out which one will best address your issues. To help you choose, here is a once-over of the stages, what they are useful for, and what a commonplace client resembles:

LinkedIn

LinkedIn is regularly the decision stage for B2B organizations, and particularly if your objective is lead age. This is likewise an ideal stage for publication content, and it can assist you with setting up your organization as a confided pioneer in your field, fabricate expert for your brand, and draw in leads through discussions.

Twitter

Twitter is the go-to stage if your business is about promptness, and if you need to contact adherents with breaking news, declarations, significant messages, and other at the time data.

Facebook

This is by a long shot the biggest stage, with more than 2 billion month-to-month dynamic clients, 61 percent of whom are Americans between the ages of 25 and 54. Facebook is useful for lead age, and its promoting stage can be exceptionally tweaked to target unmistakable crowds.

Pinterest

Images are the name of the game when it comes to Pinterest, and this platform is great if you are looking to drive sales because over 90 percent of users plan purchases using the platform.

Social media is an indispensable tool for any business that wants to remain pertinent and gain exposure online, because not only can it connect you with prospects that are right next door, but it can also help you reach out to people all across the globe. Online media is likewise a fantastic apparatus for building brand awareness, finding new leads, producing more site traffic, becoming acquainted with your crowd better, picking up knowledge into the shopping propensities for your best clients, and in any event, improving your client care. The secret to picking the correct online media stage for your business is tied in with affirming the objectives you need to accomplish through web-based media advertising, sorting out what stages your intended interest group is on and picking a stage that matches with the kind of content you make.

4.2 Leveraging a Social Media Influencer Model for Content Marketing

Whether or not you are a business-to-business firm focusing on top heads or a business to consumer brand pursuing recent college grads, your crowd is via online media. With generally 2.6 billion month-to-month active online media clients currently, the number is simply going to ascend in the coming years. Also, the most ideal approach to develop your business is to adequately connect with this steadily developing crowd via web-based media.

The main issue is that most organizations either do not use their web-based media profiles to their maximum capacity, or in the correct route for computerized promoting. Famous, inadequate, and amateur systems that include showering and imploring your content on various channels will not do a lot of good.

For a definitive upper hand, it is significant that you influence your online media content showcasing adequately. Upgraded content promoting matched with an essential online media approach is an incredible mix one that will amplify your computerized marketing return on investment. To help kick you off, here are a couple of tips to help you influence web-based media content showcasing successfully:

1. Upgrade Content for Each Platform

It is not sufficient to just distinguish and post on the correct web-based media stages. It is similarly significant that you post the correct sort of content that is most appropriate for every stage. The crowds on every stage have their desires and inclinations for what they need to see on it. While Facebook turns out best for curated content and recordings, Instagram is for photographs and stories. Twitter is for news, GIFs, and blog entries; at that point LinkedIn is best for organization news, work related content, and expert content.

2. Post on Relevant Social Networks

Organizations frequently accept they should be ubiquitous and make social profiles on everything from LinkedIn to Snapchat. Although, there truly is not any requirement for them to do as such. Particularly if your intended interest group does not have a presence on the stages you are posting content on. While there are various advantages to every online media application, putting time and cash in ones that will not give you the sort of return on investment you need would be a waste. Sort out which stages adjust well to your business, and afterward put all your energy into taking advantage of them.

3. Be Consistent in Your Social Media Content Marketing

Consistency is fundamental to be fruitful in online media content promoting. Posting content consistently can help you increment your crowd commitment and reach. You should likewise be predictable in your content, tone, and the style of your brand over all of your interpersonal applications. Consistency in content conveyance will assist with building your brand personality and increment brand awareness. Try to make a presenting plan on how to assist you with looking after consistency in your content. You can utilize web-based media tools for management or stages to computerize posting accordingly on your content schedule.

4. Draw in Followers

Since you are reliably distributing improved content on the correct stages, take your game to the following level by connecting with your crowd.

The most ideal approach to naturally become your online media reach is to associate with your devotees and influencers.

In two ongoing reports from the Content Marketing Institute, they found that 91% of business to business and 86% of business to consumer advertisers plan on utilizing content showcasing in their advanced missions.

Everybody needs a bit of the pie. By committing some time every day to interfacing with your crowd, you will dominate your opposition. You can like your supporters' posts and pages on Facebook, or express gratitude toward them in the remarks when they share your posts or retweet you. Online media content showcasing is tied in with producing enduring associations with your adherents. Even the smallest things go a long way to establish brand loyalty.

5. Pay to Promote Your Posts

The natural reach of online media content, all things considered, is dead. The times of basically posting content via online media and getting changes are finished. To expand your return on investment, you need to use paid advancements in your web-based media content showcasing. Paid notices help you target explicit crowd gatherings that would read your content. This expands your range, perceivability, and brand awareness. A paid ad generally includes a call-to-action button within the ad creative. By following crowd reactions and commitment rates on your advertisements, you can enhance your campaigns for better results.

When it comes investigation and advancement, there are two interesting points, and they are both interlinked. Initially, it is significant that you consistently investigate your online media content advertising measurements to infer helpful experiences about your web-based media movement. By sorting out what is working, and what is not, you will spare important assets and increment your return on investment.

The subsequent interesting point here is not just your own effort, yet additionally that of your influencers. It is insufficient to just work together with influencers. To capitalize on your influencer marketing program, you need the correct influencers.

Fighting the temptation to advance and discuss your brand via online media is a test. Yet, web-based media content advertising is tied in with making content that the clients will discover accommodating when they are prepared to settle on a buy choice. Regardless of how great you think your online media content showcasing procedures are, there are consistently ways you can improve. Utilizing these tips, you can use your web-based media presence to improve your marking.

4.3 Alternative Content Promotion Techniques

Marketers spend endless hours looking for ways they can reach their target audience. Accordingly, the test in this is that a greater number of times than not customary strategies can be troublesome and a sluggish cycle. To make a quick sprinkle in beginning a business or divulging another item, you should create revenue in extraordinary and some of the time whimsical ways, for example, utilizing elective techniques for showcasing. Consequently, when done effectively you can make an individual association with your intended interest group. All things considered, who does not very much want to feel like they are getting customized messaging?

Some people have so much success with their content marketing strategies that they have hundreds of thousands of readers. Of course, great content is a big part of the equation, but the other often overlooked area of content marketing is content promotion.

This post will cover some of the more advanced techniques for promoting your content. The most successful content marketers use them, and they are reaping all of the rewards. Here is how you can attract scores of new visitors with your content:

1. Lifestyle Marketing

Lifestyle promoting includes connecting with clients in a casual setting and pinpointing their diversions through your messaging. For example, included in this which many of you may already do without knowing is interacting with your customers at places such as farmer's markets, festivals, and other places where there are a large number of customers at once. Furthermore, possible clients at these spots in all likelihood have a couple of comparative leisure activities or interests. Also, it is essential to gain by these interests and give expected clients something of significant worth. For example, Red Bull does a great job of marketing their products at events such as extreme sports, where many people are much more likely to drink their products.

2. Product Placement

Product placement includes embedding your brand or item into some sort of media. For example, this could be any visual-based promotion. It is a far and wide faith in the showcasing scene that items or brands set in commercials will prompt expanded awareness and radiate an uplifting mentality towards the brand. Most importantly, this does not need to be done for an enormous scope, you can begin nearby and perceive how awareness for your item increments.

3. Buzz Marketing

Buzz marketing, also known as word-of-mouth marketing focuses on customers passing along information. Now you already may be asking how you can implement this if it relies on my customers.

There are a few preconditions of buzz advertising for it to accurately work. To begin with, your item should be either one of a kind, new, or better than the opposition. Second, your brand should stick out. Third, your publicizing should be noteworthy, interesting, extraordinary, and novel. Finally, you need to get the purchaser engaged with your brand.

Likewise, using appropriate marking practices can give you a paramount, strong picture all through all of your channels that presents your item as better than the rest. Accordingly, when this insight is joined with a customized, predictable brand message you will have the option to make a buzz for your brand.

4. Experimental Marketing

Experimental advertising is a mix of direct showcasing, field advertising, and deals advancements. Instead of just parting with free samples this strategy targets drawing in with clients at different areas or occasions. For instance, offering guests of a festival a sample of your product first, and pitching them on why it should be valued by them is a perfect example of this. If the product is desired after, the customer can be offered a discount or an add-on for interacting and trying out the product.

There are a couple of steps to ensure this is compelling. To start with, you should pick a reasonable market portion to target. Second, pick the opportune time and spot to connect with clients. Third, guarantee the experience speaks to the brand in a positive light towards clients.

5. Guerilla Marketing

Guerrilla promoting utilizes elective strategies and settings to discover imaginative methods of getting things done.

This strategy functions admirably when you have restricted assets or need to grow your showcasing without extending your spending plan.

In this manner, with the utilization of media, publicizing, advertising, and surprises you can arrive at your clients with individual correspondence that hits near and dear. Above all, assembling a relationship with your clients should be the objective of guerrilla showcasing. In addition, by getting them to react a certain way there is a greater chance that your messaging will turn them into loyal brand ambassadors.

An ongoing online media closure shows the significance of utilizing numerous types of advertising for your business. Online media advertising is a valuable special instrument. Indeed, numerous organizations pick up reputation utilizing locales like Facebook, Instagram, Twitter and Pinterest. While web-based media will probably stay a feasible alternative for conveying messages to your objective market, it very well might be in your organization's wellbeing to enhance advertising efforts. It is critical to reach consumers through a variety of channels to reinforce brand recognition and drive conversions. Each channel supports the others and compounds, almost exponentially, the results for your brand.

All together for your content advertising procedure to succeed, you need to expand your advancement efforts. The techniques sketched out above are similar procedures utilized by the best content advertisers on the planet. Presently it is your chance to fabricate a major crowd.

4.4 Measuring the Impact of Your Social Media Marketing

Social Media is ubiquitous and most brands understand the importance of having an active social media presence due to this. As such, marketers spend quite a big proportion of their budget on social media. However, while it is everywhere, social media is still considered to be quite a new platform. The means that all the social media theory, best practices, thought leadership and experts are not as established as they are when it comes to other forms of marketing. Unfortunately, this means that many marketers or business owners are not exactly sure on where to begin, or how to best use the data available to them.

An issue that stems from this for many people does not know how to prove the impact of their social media campaigns in a clear and quantitative manner. A few advertisers evaluate the accomplishment of web-based media regarding likes, shares, re-tweets, devotees, endorsers, etc. Others go to Google Analytics and take a look at the measure of direct traffic that their web-based media stages are bringing to their site and additionally bringing about a change. In any case, there is no uncertainty that numerous individual's ledge neglect to quantify the adequacy of their web-based media crusades.

A basic piece of web-based media promoting, similar to all of advanced advertising, is estimating the effect your online efforts make to your main concern and brand value. Every web-based media stage has its own special arrangement of measurements, alongside some widespread measurements, for example, impressions that can be followed over all stages. These stages have likewise advanced to have extensive investigation dashboards that can be handily gotten to screen insights. Following are the techniques that you can use to measure the impact:

1. Twitter Analytics

While Twitter analytics are not as comprehensive as the ones available on Facebook, you can still obtain several useful social media metrics from the platform's analytical dashboard that are worth tracking. As a preview, the stage gives you information on the quantity of tweets conveyed by your brand, the tweet impressions they procured, the visits your brand profile got, the quantity of notices your brand got and the distinction in the quantity of supporters you have month on month. For example, an increase in tweet impressions and profile visits provides an indication that the brand is attracting new and existing customers to its messaging with quality content and an increased frequency of tweeting.

Furthermore, Twitter likewise furnishes you with your top tweets and notices so you know the kind of content that draws in your adherents and the powerful supporters you ought to connect with. You can tap on any tweet on this screen to see more itemized measurements. Talking about commitment, Twitter has accurate measurements on commitment worth following. It gives a brand their commitment rate on the stage, to give a comprehension of if the brand messaging is resounding with clients to make a move constantly along the business venture.

2. Google Analytics for Social Media

While all the web-based media stages have a few normal and novel measurements worth following, for example, impressions, commitment, communications and socioeconomics, the genuine effect of your web-based media advertising can likewise be estimated by the traffic measurements accessible on the Google Analytics of your website.

You can additionally quantify the social traffic by every stage when you click into the social tab. With this depth of understanding, you can easily identify the top traffic acquisition medium, the behavior of the traffic from each medium and their effect on the business goals of a website.

3. Instagram Analytics

Investigation on Instagram is separated into three classes: information on the action on your profile, information on the content you are posting and information on your adherents or crowd. Dissimilar to Facebook and Twitter, however, Instagram does not offer month to month correlation information however offers week by week examinations all things being equal. In the activity section of your analytics, analyzing the interactions your Instagram profile has had is key. These set of insights measure the actions people take when they engage with your brand online.

4. Facebook Analytics

Of all the web-based media stages, Facebook offers the most thorough investigation that can be seen on your page's experiences area, just as be remotely downloaded. Inside the review part of the experiences, you can see information on activities taken on the page, online visits, page sneak peaks, page likes, post reach, post commitment and much more. The top-level and priority metrics to keep an eye on include page views, post reach and post engagements. These three define how your brand is performing on Facebook to reach new customers and to retain the attention of existing and potential customers towards your messaging.

- Post reach is the number of times individuals see your posts on their Facebook timetable. This can be natural or paid and is separated in like manner.

- Post commitments are the number of times individuals have drawn in with your posts through preferences, remarks, shares and clicking. This encourages you to distinguish if the posts you are putting out are fascinating to your supporters or not.

- Site hits are the complete number of times individuals have visited your page and effectively put forth an attempt to investigate your brand on the web.

The posts tab likewise gives you data on how each post on your Facebook page performed dependent on the scope and commitment it got. This knowledge can be helpful in fundamentally assessing your content technique and changing it to improve brand execution on the web. Likewise, under the individuals tab, you can see the socioeconomics of the individuals who follow your page and who you frequently reach to modify content further to build commitment and significance. You would now be able to check if your fans are recent college grads from metropolitan urban areas or children of post war America from the nation, accordingly, adjusting the brand messaging to speak to them.

Examining your web-based media execution measurements and insights is presently simpler than any time in recent memory. Maybe, more significant, is to distinguish which measurements truly mirror your business objectives and merging the information into noteworthy promoting reports. This is the place where an office can step in, characterize your objectives and track significant execution against it.

Chapter 5: Insights of Facebook, Instagram, YouTube, Twitter, LinkedIn, and Snapchat

Online media is steadily evolving. There is consistently another insane way individuals can archive each part of their lives, however imagine a scenario where you are a business. With so numerous web-based media locales effectively out there and significantly additionally springing up every day, where do you start? Do you make a Facebook account or do you bounce on whatever "the new Pinterest" is today?

Using web-based media in your business procedure is perhaps the most ideal approaches to get your name out there. It is an extraordinary method to advertise your administrations, items, and help support your brand. Not just that, it allows you to interface with fans, clients, and forthcoming clients on a closer to home, human level. Beneath, we all separate every stage and assist you with figuring out how to make the most out of it for your business.

1. Twitter

Twitter is relentless, succinct, and simple approach to associate with your crowd. With more than 310 million enrolled clients, Twitter is an ocean of data of 140 character or less content holding on to be perused, clicked, followed, and re-tweeted. Twitter produces more than 175 million tweets day by day and permits you to share brisk snippets of data and photographs with an end goal to drive individuals back to your site or points of arrival. You just get a limited quantity of characters, so make the most of them.

When showcasing on Twitter, you need to have content that is alluring enough for individuals to stop and navigate. Individuals are typically looking through rapidly so it takes something beyond straightforward content to leave them speechless.

Ensure when you are building your tweets, you are making individuals need to navigate. Try utilizing statements, measurements, or questions identified with the connection you are tweeting as an approach to individuals needing to understand more. Consolidate photographs, surveys, GIFs, or even short recordings. While Twitter is an incredible method to share fast contemplations and create traffic to your site and offers, it is critical to ensure you are likewise constructing associations with supporters.

Individuals follow you since they like what you state, however regularly additionally take part in discussions. Like you would on Facebook, ask and react to inquiries, react to makes reference to and direct messages. Twitter is as valuable for driving traffic for what it is worth for client care.

2. Facebook

With about 2.38 billion month-to-month dynamic clients worldwide as of April 2019, Facebook is one of the most famous stages, for individual use as well as business too. For organizations, Facebook is a spot to share photographs, updates, and general news with the individuals who follow or like you. Fanatics of your business go to your Facebook page to discover what is new with your organization, see photos of what is happening, or investigate occasions.

Whenever you have made a solid following it is imperative to utilize notices or photographs to share your items, offers, administrations. You should likewise post things that get your crowd to draw in with your posts.

3. LinkedIn

LinkedIn is unique in relation to the remainder of the web-based media sources since it is particularly intended for business and experts.

Clients principally go to LinkedIn to exhibit their professional training and expert musings, making it one of the more significant stages to use for those in business to business. Between features like LinkedIn Pulse, Company Pages, InMail, Groups, and the capacity to see who has seen your own profile, LinkedIn is a significant device for driving traffic, however prospecting, building up idea authority, just as selecting.

4. Pinterest

Pinterest is one of the most special showcasing stages. Rather than posting content for your crowd to peruse, on Pinterest, you are posting simply an interactive picture and a short subtitle. This is a mainstream stage for brands with a substantial item, for example attire and food brands, eateries, those in e-commerce, and so forth. Pinterest is a shallow stage, so every picture you present has on be high-caliber and striking to hang out in your feed. When you begin posting pictures ensure they connect back to a connected blog or page on your site. As individuals navigate from your picture to your site they need to see or peruse something that is identified with the picture that got their attention.

When you start posting sort out your Pinterest by isolating it into sheets. Each board ought to have a classification comparative with various parts of your business. Make it basic for your devotees to discover what they are searching for. Likewise ensure that your subtitle is catchphrase upgraded. Like some other web index, Pinterest cannot slither pictures. This subtitle is the means by which your pin will show up when individuals are perusing.

5. YouTube

YouTube is the main video-sharing stage on the planet. On your channel, your brand can share and alter its own recordings, make playlists, and brief conversations.

Since it was purchased over by Google in 2006, YouTube is another stage that the inquiry offers need to in its list items so exploit it.

YouTube for your business is an incredible method to get your face out there. Recordings are significantly more captivating and shareable than text content and they additionally help your inquiry rank in Google. While making recordings for YouTube quality issues. Ensure there is a reason and incentive to what exactly you are transferring and sharing. Additionally, try to focus on your creation esteem. Both the video and sound of what you transfer should be fresh, clear, and straightforward.

Now that you know how important social media marketing is for your business and what some of the most popular platforms have to offer, it is time for you to put it to use.

5.1 Marketing Budget of Various Social Media Accounts

Each business little, medium, or huge and ought to have a social methodology, and each technique should be upheld by a web-based media financial plan. Planning encourages you guarantee you will have the assets to accomplish your objectives, regardless of whether that is advancing another business or driving deals on another brand. Furthermore, without a precise online media advertising spending plan, it is difficult to know the genuine return on investment of your work.

Before choosing the amount of your promoting financial plan to designate to social, research your clients and decide how web-based media will assist you with accomplishing your marketing destinations.

For example, if a huge level of your business comes from the Internet, it might bode well for your brand to spend more via web-based media than print, communicated, standard mail, or other advertising channels.

There is nothing of the sort as a one size fits all web-based media financial plan. Each organization has various assets and various needs. Yet, regardless of whether you are working with a shoestring or comfortable financial plan, these are the key parts you should consider along with your counts. These are the core components you should include in your social media marketing budget.

1. **Software and Tools**

Prepare your online media spending plan with these tools and software. Use Google AdWords to research and offer on applicable catchphrases. This can likewise be utilized to educate your social substance methodology. Your site, microsites, and points of arrival should be facilitated. A portion of these facilitating suppliers incorporate space names that should be bought, as well. Makers convey brand resources, yet it is valuable to have instruments, for example, Adobe Creative Cloud in-house for different altering needs, from picture resizing, to applying marking. Stages like Trello or Wrike can assist with smoothing out creation and venture the executives in the background. We are clearly inclined toward Hootsuite, particularly on account of now is the ideal time sparing booking capacities. Apparatuses like Marketo and MailChimp can assist with email showcasing and that is only the tip of the iceberg. Track your web-based media crusades with apparatuses like Hootsuite Analytics.

2. **Content Creation**

Content is and consistently will be above all else. Furthermore, accordingly, it should represent a critical part of your financial plan.

Numerous social advertisers spend the greater part of their online media financial plan on content creation alone.

3. Paid Advertising

All social media strategies should include organic content and if your budget allows paid advertising. Every social media channel offers marketers ways to boost posts or run full-fledged campaigns.

4. Paid partnerships

From influencer advertising to co-marked missions, cushion your online media spending plan with space for paid organizations. Following are two types of advertising procedures

- Co-branded campaigns: They may not need more financing for content than a typical campaign, yet they will request association and arranging time from the fitting work force.

- Influencer campaign: Online media impact rates can change; however, you can utilize this essential recipe as a benchmark for your financial plan. From Instagram's partner tag feature, to YouTube influencer organizations, there are numerous joint effort prospects your organization should spending plan for.

5. Management

While there are instruments or rethinking alternatives for web-based media the board, it is acceptable practice to have at any rate one individual in-house overseeing social at any rate part of the time. Online media directors or groups should manage:

- Procedure and examination

- Online media the board (planning, distributing, and commitment)

- Content creation
- Crowd exploration and development
- Missions and advancements
- Network the board

6. Training

There are loads of free online media preparing assets out there, yet it is consistently advantageous to put resources into preparing for your group. Contingent upon your group's ability levels and mission needs, these are a couple of preparing alternatives you ought to consider remembering for your web-based media spending plan:

- Blueprint Live: While Facebook's one-day workshops are right now greeting just, watch out for join alternatives later on. In the interim, consider Blueprint accreditation courses or free Blueprint e-learning classes.

- Hootsuite Academy: From single courses to declaration programs, Hootsuite Academy offers an inventory of courses instructed by industry geniuses and customized for organizations.

- LinkedIn Learning: LinkedIn's people group is an objective segment for your business; these online courses might be beneficial.

While making your budget, make sure to keep all the above points in mind.

5.2 Standing Out from Others on Social Media

With countless individuals and organizations now active via web-based media, it very well may be a touch of overpowering attempting to concoct approaches to slice through all the commotion. Yet, on the other hand, in some cases the appropriate responses are directly in front of us and no you do not really require a viral hit to stick out. Following are a few things you need to follow to stand apart from others:

1. Have a Strategy in Mind

Well having a methodology will provide you guidance for content, and save time to get innovative. A procedure will guarantee your group is on the same wavelength and that nothing is escaping from anybody's sight. You will be completely ready for what is coming up, and you will have the opportunity to tissue out imaginative and viable approaches to spread the news and make superb content to help your drives.

2. Use Network Tools

Another approach to help your business stand apart via online media is to utilize network apparatuses to add some additional oomph to your quality. Make certain to utilize diverse posting methods and content types as such, become accustomed to stirring up recordings, pictures, and remember to toss plain content posts into your content plan. Jump into how each organization works and investigate features like Twitter surveys, Twitter records, different picture posts, live recordings, Instagram Stories and Live Stories and whatever different apparatuses may be available to you for a particular web-based media network.

3. Use Strong Visuals

A decent, basic approach to help your business stand apart via online media is to use solid visuals. Keep pictures and video as clear and high caliber as you can. Having the option to convey your branding and mirror the vibe of your brand through imaging can be vital to pulling in and holding adherents. Make sure to get inventive and investigate approaches to utilize visuals in surprising manners for instance attempting puzzle feeds, and network pictures on Instagram.

4. Use your Brand Voice

One of the quickest and easiest ways to help your business stand out on social media is to be yourself. Although nailing your brand voice can be quite the process, it will help you stand out from the competition, and subsequently attract the right followers to your social channels.

5. Write Compelling Captions

Try to make your captions compelling, while adding value to your audience. Remember that the point is to connect with your audience so try creating conversations instead of just speaking.

6. Create Recurring Posts

One surefire way to help your brand or business stand out on social is to create a recurring post or event. Perhaps host a weekly Q & A livestream on the social media network of your choosing, or share a weekly tip, or create a best of the week slideshow. The key is to create something that keeps fans coming back, week after week. This method can be one of the best ways to get creative, connect with your audience, add value, and even show a little personality

7. Theme Your Accounts

Theming your accounts is a great way to boost your presence especially on Instagram.

Theming essentially means sticking to a distinct color palette or approach, using the same filters and the like to create a distinct look and feel.

Hopefully these points will help you spark some creative ideas which you can implement with your brand or business. At the end of the day social media is not a sprint, it is a marathon, and showing up and being consistent is key to success.

5.3 Creating Attraction through Your Content on Social Media

Online media is an extraordinary method to associate with your guests; however, accomplishment via web-based media takes a ton of time and exertion. Attractions frequently start off with the best goals, but after a while accounts are forgotten, and social media takes a back seat. Regardless of whether you have quite recently begun a record or need to take your current efforts to the following level, these valuable tips will assist you with drawing in your intended interest group.

1. Be Consistent

Content promoting and overseeing web-based media records can take a lot of time, bigger attractions have groups devoted to their records and creating their content. In the event that you have a little advertising group or it is simply you, dealing with all the records and creating content consistently can at times feel stressing. An incredible spot to begin is to put aside an hour seven days to design your online media content. Consider effective things that your crowd would discover important as well as intriguing. Then set aside another few hours in the week to produce this content. For Facebook and Twitter, posting three times each week is a great beginning.

2. Monitor Your Accounts

A significant piece of any promoting procedure is to screen and assess how well it is functioning. You would prefer not to go through a few hours on something that is not profiting your business. Essentially, in the event that you can see that something is working and is intriguing to your crowd, you need to proceed with that. Take a look at the bits of knowledge and examination from your online media records to perceive what posts your crowd is drawing in with. Assess why the ones with the best commitment work, and why the ones with the least commitment do not. Watch that your content is drawing in, significant and mirrors your brand.

3. Identify Your Audience

Contemplating your crowd, and what they truly need to see, will help you with regards to setting up your record. By chance that you need a little assistance, think about taking a look at a contender's page to perceive what is functioning admirably for them. Bigger attractions are particularly useful for motivation, as they have presumably as of now put away the time and cash needed to sort it out. An overall general guideline for attractions is that the two pictures and recordings make great content, yet that recordings regularly get better commitment.

4. Take Risks

Most brands have a Facebook page, and the majorities also have a Twitter account. Almost all of them post photos because this is the easiest type of content to get out there. So, mix it up a little and go for something different. If you are using Facebook, consider including some video content as it is likely to get you more views than a photo, and it is more visually stimulating.

5. Timing

Consider when your target audience is likely to be online. Most important of all, experiment. Every page is unique, and it is not unusual to discover an optimal time for posting that you just cannot explain. Once you have settled on times, remembering to post on schedule can be difficult luckily; there are plenty of tools available to do the remembering for you. Facebook has its own built-in scheduling tool, and there are many other options to cover all bases. Once you have your content ready, just create and schedule your posts and they will go out automatically.

Social media is more important than ever for attractions, with those considering their next day out increasingly looking to their friends and influencers for inspiration. Regularly popping up in the social feed of your target audience and sharing interesting content that makes them smile is the perfect way to remain front-of-mind.

5.4 Leveraging Social Media to Sell Your Bran

Brand dedication is characterized as the inclination of a shopper toward one business or item over another, and it can genuinely represent the deciding moment of a brand. It drives in-store traffic, visits to your site, verbal suggestions, and the transformation of clients. This implies the distinction among benefits and misfortunes. Also, as a rule, in the present interconnected world, brand steadfastness relies upon your capacity to use the intensity of web-based media to fabricate associations with your customers and clients.

You most likely have a marketing system, a showcasing technique, and a rundown of extra miniature methodologies. In any case, if you do not have a social methodology, you need to characterize that rapidly. Social media is no longer just about posting and not engaging.

Online media is promoting, showcasing, correspondences and selling all wrapped up into one compelling and unimaginably productive medium. It needs a devoted showcasing and correspondence system, much the same as your different channels.

Obviously, you will probably sell. However, you cannot be unmitigated about it via online media. Show, do not tell. Weave a visual story around your brand; however, do not forcefully sell your items or administrations. Great narrating will assist you with associating your intended interest groups.

Online media is where your crowds can straightforwardly connect with you. Urge them to remark on and share your posts via web-based media. Be available to their inquiries and ensure you are reacting obligingly to the entirety of their remarks. Attempt to react to them at the earliest opportunity. You need to assemble a two-way channel with the goal that you can procure the trust of your clients.

Another extraordinary method of utilizing online media for business is to team up with important web-based media influencers. Not exclusively would they be able to assist with making buzz about your brand yet in addition construct your believability. This thus, can really assist you with getting transformations. Eventually, your social procedure is about client support. Clients will regularly go to web-based media when they have had both positive and negative encounters. It is dependent upon you to fix whatever the issues might be. The most exceedingly awful thing you can do is overlook these issues.

You may have incredible content and fascinating items to feature. Nonetheless, basically posting them via online media is not in every case adequate. You need to likewise ensure it contacts the correct crowds and educates them.

However, tossing some cash in, and anticipating that it should do wonders for you will not work. You need to see how promotions chip away at online media. Attempt to comprehend your crowd socioeconomics and focus on your advertisements to explicit clients. Really at that time would you be able to anticipate some great outcomes.

You need to begin by making clear principles and desires for your group. Start preparing workers on the most proficient method to utilize web-based media in manners that satisfy your brand guidelines. You ought to have a group of individuals who can react and draw in with clients and fans when they have questions, concerns, or are voicing their assessment.

Regardless of whether you do have a negative client, a positive client care insight on social can totally turn that around. Furthermore, remember that via web-based media, others are watching to perceive how you react, so it is essential to ensure it is a snappy turnaround with an accommodating reaction to the client. The nature of your client care assumes a major part in deciding how individuals feel about your brand. Ensure that you are demonstrating your clients a similar encounter both on the web and when offline.

5.5 A Career Perspective of Social Media

A large number of individuals utilize web-based media consistently. 72% of all Internet clients are via online media. Furthermore, social media is not, at this point simply a stage for speaking with your school flat mate or your grandmother. Individuals, associations and organizations everywhere on the world can see your action via online media. Furthermore, the individuals you work for or who are thinking about employing you? They are looking.

Your web-based media presence is the means by which you introduce yourself to the world and that incorporates current and future bosses. Your online media presence is regularly the initial introduction you make on possible businesses. In case you are attempting to land a meeting, get employed, or even development in your present profession, web-based media matters. Is web-based media harming your profession possibilities or would it be able to really help you land your fantasy work?

Your web-based media profile should not be as spruced up as your resume. Yet, it should in any case be proficient. Try not to post whatever expected businesses or employing chiefs would discover off-putting. This incorporates references to medications or liquor, vulgar posts or photographs, and negative remarks about past managers, just as bigoted, chauvinist or in any case oppressive comments.

Sift through your profiles to ensure you do not have anything you ought to erase. Also, make sure to go route back. A significant number of us have had a similar web-based media profiles for quite a long time, and you may not need expected bosses to consider you the similar way your secondary school schoolmates did. Additionally, consider what posts and pictures you like and remark on, as these can likewise appear on your profile and influence how you are seen. Try to eliminate, un-tag, or shroud any substance you do not need found.

Online media gives businesses a new, unique gander at an up-and-comer. Also, web-based media can even be utilized to grandstand characteristics that do not really have a place on a resume. Utilize your social profiles to flaunt your novel character, your awareness of what is actually funny, or your magnanimous nature.

Try not to avoid posting (socially sensitive) jokes, thoughts on culture or recent developments, or photographs of you running that 5k or assisting with that Habitat for Humanity fabricate. All things considered; bosses need to recruit genuine individuals that they will appreciate working with not hyper proficient online media bots. Furthermore, regardless of whether your exercises via online media do not make you resemble a holy person or qualify you for the following Nobel Prize, social profiles can even now be utilized to show that you are a balanced, intriguing individual.

If you go through hours playing chess, share your advantage by preferring or sharing chess-related things. Your employing administrator will see that you have enthusiasm, just as the capacity to think basically and settle on educated choices. If you love sewing and make your own scarves, caps and tea warmers, utilize a social stage to show your imagination.

Remember that while web-based media offers you the occasion to brand and market yourself on the web, you are likewise simultaneously a saleable item for these organizations. An alarming pattern is the obscured line between who precisely online media organizations are serving. They offer administrations to up-and-comers looking for presentation. Simultaneously, they forcefully market and offer admittance to organizations to promote or upgrade admittance.

Second to the goal of reaching passive candidates for corporations who have a social media presence is the mission to brand and sell. A multimillion-dollar global executive search firm site recently updated their registration process to include applying via LinkedIn. The fine print noted that when the candidate applied that way, he or she was granting access to their entire LinkedIn connection database to that recruitment company.

While online media can help you advance your vocation by introducing your capabilities to a wide crowd, it is best drawn closer with a very much idea out methodology. You have command over your own showcasing plan, and web-based media can offer you the source where to execute it.

One thing is clear web-based media is setting down deep roots. And keeping in mind that web-based media is incredible for making individual associations, it can likewise be utilized to propel your expert objectives. Put somewhat thought into your web-based media presence and activities, and you could see large returns. Putting all the theory into practice is the most valuable way to prove your proficiency. If you are starting out on your own then social media can become your best companion. Social media could even be the key to the next big step in your career. Get tangled in the world of social media and start succeeding easily and effectively by using the least efforts possible.

Conclusion

Social Media has been of great help to many of the individuals residing in your surroundings. If you take a look at the society today that we live in, we can easily see how social media has made many normal looking individuals turn into stars. It can really turn your life upside down if you start to use it efficiently. Today, social media is not just confined to Facebook or Twitter. Today, social media comprises of many applications that you can use to succeed. And the fun thing is that, each social media application has its own target audience and each needs a different sort of treatment to help you succeed.

This book is all about building your own personal brand in this modern age of social media. Branding may look very difficult to you because currently, you may think who would even consider you for any sort of thing, but trust me social media is the king of all. Mastering the social media tricks and tips to succeed you can easily become the best in the game. With social media by your side, nothing is impossible anymore. Within, the span of a couple of months of hard work and should we change the word to "smart work" you can become the best in town.

In this book, we gave you a detailed outlook on the importance of social media, the different social media platforms available to you presently and what actually is social media marketing. Content creation is a pretty easy job with the correct information and appropriate tools. Content creation is not a new tern for those who may consider it as a new term, the detailed history of social media is also discussed in the chapters above. You can create content but without content marketing it can end up completely useless.

Social Media has been the talk of the book; you can start earning with help of social media once you start converting your personal social media into business social media. You can start posting the best posts once you have read this book by the help of the amazing techniques detailed in the chapters. Now, success mainly depends upon the content you create and which platform are you using to sell your content on, if the two variables do not sync together then you are doing it all wrong. Marketing budget, impact measuring and other alternative content promoting techniques are also discussed in this book that you can take an advantage of for your brand.

Well, it is pretty clear; master the art of social media and content creation and you will find success at your door step. Do not wait any further, it is your time to succeed, so start branding but start branding in the right way using social media as your best partner.

www.ingramcontent.com/pod-product-compliance
Lightning Source LLC
LaVergne TN
LVHW050149060326
832904LV00003B/78